ORIGINAL PUBLICATIONS
New York

PAPA JIM'S HERBAL MAGIC WORKBOOK
By Papa Jim

© ORIGINAL PUBLICATIONS 2001

ISBN: 0-942272-64-1

FIRST EDITION
First Printing 2001

Cover art by Raul Canizares

Original Publications
P.O. Box 236
Old Bethpage, New York 11804-0236
(516) 454-6809

Printed in the United States of America

HERBAL MAGIC

Long before the days of science, man was at a loss to explain the things of the earth. With no actual knowledge to guide them, men were forced to turn to mythical explanations of the various elements. To them the sun was a flowery chariot, thunder was the angry wrath of a certain god. Likewise the existence of various herbs, roots, shrubs and flowers were explained as the result of the activities of the various gods and goddesses.

As man grew in mental stature, other herbs and roots were discovered to have certain healing or medicinal values. Still later, men began to ascribe powers to the roots and herbs which were believed to be in direct proportion to their likeness to the various parts of the human body. This practice was known as the doctrine of signatures. The practice was widely followed during medieval times. Many of the discoveries made then are still in use today, not because of the resemblance of the herb to a part of the human body but because the herb men, quite by accident, found some rather valuable remedies.

Because of the earlier associations of herbs, roots and flowers with religious practices, the use of them for a practical purpose was needlessly retarded. Men considered it a sacrilege to put these plants to work for them as cures for their ills. Many plants could not be touched except by those delegated to handle them.

Those who have studied the history of herbs maintain that it is in reality a history of mankind. So interwoven with human activities are the histories of the various herbs that the changes in man's conception of nature are recorded in them.

Proof of the ancient's use of herbs is contained in the Ebers Papyrus which is older than the Book of Exodus. Prescriptions listed in this ancient papyrus contain more than a dozen common herbs used extensively at that time, 1500 B.C. Hippocrates used more than four hundred herbs in his practice of medicine.

Many of the early herb formulae were guarded secrets and could be purchased only by extremely wealthy persons. Some contained as many as a hundred different ingredients.

Knowledge of the use of herbs for all sorts of purposes was spread from one country to another by explorers, voyagers and armies. From the East the knowledge was taken to the Moors, thence to Spain and Portugal. From these countries the knowledge spread north to France, Switzerland, Britain and other countries. Each country added to the original knowledge until the complete use of herbs and roots was a complicated and highly specialized practice.

With this rich background of use through the centuries, is it any wonder that in many parts of the world the use of roots and herbs is still prevalent? Is it any wonder that some persons still ascribe to these plants a power which they cannot possibly possess?

Herbs were extensively used during the period when Black Magic was practiced. Without them, it is claimed, Black Magic could not have flourished. The concoctions which were used were each supposed to bring about a definite result. Monkshood was used to produce fever; Nightshade was said to make the eater see ghosts; Black Hellebore disturbed the nervous system and caused swellings; Eyebright brought on rheumatism; Henbane caused convulsions. One had but to pay a price to bring these misfortunes upon his enemies. Whether the herbs actually caused the conditions for which they were sold history does not tell us.

Flowers were generally associated with sunshine and fairies. Their origins were attributed to finer, more pleasant happenings. The Cowslip was said to be the key to heaven, Anemone was a fairy shelter. For this reason flowers became the symbols with which witches and evil spirits were frequently driven away or held in check.

It It is impossible to give a complete list of all the herbs, roots, flowers, shrubs and trees which have held an important place in the lives of men through the centuries. To do so would require many volumes. Instead we will note those which were considered most important and which were generally used. Also we will list many of those which are still in use in various parts of the world.

METHODS OF USING HERBS
FOR MAGICAL PURPOSES

PREPARING HERBAL TEAS

INFUSION: Is a term for an herb tea designed for a purpose. Teas are commonly made by pouring hot water over the leaves or flowers, 2 cups of water to one cup of herbs, let it stand for 15 minutes, and if you want to drink it you can add honey. If using it to sprinkle, just sprinkle.

DECOTION: When making a tea with roots, barks, or stems, these are the hard parts of the herbs, they must be boiled. You can a either tie them in a clean cloth or just put them in the water. Put the roots in the water before putting the water to boil, after the water starts to boil, add the leaves, leave set for 10 minutes.

When you are finished with the leaves and stems, sprinkle them around your property, for good luck, do not throw them in the garbage.

PREPARING HERBAL BATHS

Baths are often used in herbal magic. Fresh herbs are hard to find, so you can use dried herbs, unless you are growing your own. Bathing allows the practitioner a simple way to maximize the success of the ritual by spreading the herb's power over the entire body. Later in the book we have included recipes combining various herbs for some very powerful baths.

1. Use the leg of a panty hose, or even better use both legs, put one leg inside the other. Then put the herbs inside the panty hose and let it hang in warm bath water. Allow the herbs to soak 15-20 minutes and your bath is ready. Squeeze the stocking several times to release the ingredients. When you enter the tub, swish the stocking around the water and rub it over your body. If you desire bubbles or suds in your bath, you may add soap to your mixture.

When you remove the hose from the tub, put it in a wide mouth jar and add more water to the jar and leave it soak over night. The following day, just pour the water into the bath, if using a shower pour the water over your head, after you have soaped and rinsed off.

1A. If you are going to take a shower, put the herbs in a container and pour hot water over them, leave them soak for about 15 minutes, strain and pour the mixture over your head in the shower, do not rinse off.

Another method of preparation...

BOILING: Bring 2 quarts of water to a boil, when the water starts to boil, add the herbs to the water, remove from the heat cover and leave sit for 15 minutes, strain and use a pint of the tea, either in bath water or pour over your head. Heating releases the herbs natural essences.

Some rituals require you to rub your body with the herbs. Do this after you have taken a bath, make sure none of the herbs will scratch you.

BURNING HERBS AS INCENSE

To create a certain vibration or energy in a particular location, be it your business, your home, your bedroom or a ritual room, many rituals call for the use of an herb as an incense. The best way to perform this type of ritual is with the use of quick lighting charcoal. One of the best known on the market today is made by *"Three Kings Company"* and is commonly available in any occult supply store. Make sure you do not burn charcoal in a glass container or in a flat metal container that will rest on the table, the coals become very hot. Place your coals in a vessel that will not have to be moved, or in a properly designed burner that will allow you to move it without burning yourself.

To prepare your herbs for use with charcoal, it is best that you grind them into flake or powder form and sprinkle it over previously lit coals every few minute during your ritual. You can also add anointing oils to your mixture, the purer the oil the better the scent. Do not be alarmed by an unpleasant scent as you burn herbs, the important result is the vibration produced by the herb. Later in the book we have included recipes for preparing some of the most commonly used incenses.

MAGICAL UTILITIES

Business
Barley
Comfrey
Goldenseal
Marigold
Shamewood
Spearmint
Squill Root
Violet Leaves
Yellow Duck Root

Clairvoyance
Angelica
Anise Seed
Bay
Bethel Root
Calendula
Celery
Dandelion
Eyebright
Mugwort
Uva Ursi

Curse an Enemy
Calamus
Chicory
Devil's Shoestring
Knot Grass
Patchouly Leaves
Skunk Cabbage
Vertivert Leaves
Witch Grass
Wormwood

Gambling
Bayberry
Chamomile
Devil's Shoestring
High John Root
Jamaica Ginger

Happiness
Catnip
Hawthorn
High John
Lavendar
Marjoram
Passion Flower
St. John's Wort
Witch Grass

Health & Healing
African Ginger
Almonds
Angelica
Basil Leaves
Cedar
Cinnamon
Eucalyptus
Fennel
High John
Hops
Horehound
Huckleberry
Juniper
Life Everlasting
Mugwort
Mullein
Rosebuds
Rue
Sarsperilla
St. John's Wort
Sassafras
Spikenard
Thyme Leaves
Tonka Beans
Valerian
Vervain
Wild Yam

Legal Matters
Buckthorn
Cascara Sagrada
Devil's Shoestring
Hydrangea Root
Lemon
Marigold
Sacred Bark

Love & Sex
Absinthe
Adam Root
Archangel Herb
Balm of Gilead
Basil
Black Cohosh
Blood Root
Catnip
Chamomile
Chickweed
Chili Pepper
Clove
Coriander
Couch Grass
Cubeb Berries
Damiana
Devil's Shoestring
Dill
Eve Root
Fennel
Gentian
Grains of Paradise
Ginger
High John Root
Jasmine
Juniper Berries
Khus Khus
Lavender
Lily
Linden Flower

Lovage
Lungwort
Magnolia
Maidenhair
Mandrake
Marigold
Mistletoe
Myrtle
Orange Blossom
Orris Root
Rhubarb
Rose Hips
Scullcap
Senna Root
Sweet Pea
Spikenard
Verbena Root
Vervain
Violet Leaves

Luck

Allspice
Aloe
Basil Leaves
Bayberry
Buckeye Root
Calamus
Chamomile
Grains of Paradise
Huckleberry
Irish Moss
Kelp
Nutmeg
Parsley
Pipsissewa
Silverweed
Snakeroot
Spikenard

Money Drawing

Alfalfa
Allspice
Bayberry
Bergamot
Cedar
Clove
Devil's Shoestring
Flax
Goldenseal
Jezebel
Lavender
May Apple
Nutmeg
Orris Root
Patchouly
Tonka Beans

Protection

Acacia
Angelica
Balm of Gilead
Barley
Basil
Black Cohosh
Blood Root
Cactus
Caraway Seeds
Catnip
Cinnamon
Clove
Elder Flowers
Mandrake
Marshmallow
May Apple
Myrtle
Pipsissewa
Rattlesnake Root

Unhexing / Jinx Removing

African Ginger
Angelica
Balm Gilead
Barley
Bay
Black Cohosh
Blood Root
Broom Tops
Caraway Seeds
Catnip
Chewing John Root
Chili Pepper
Galangal
Huckleberry
Hydrangea
Marjoram
Slippery Elm
Vertivert
Wahoo Bark

A

ABSINTHE

ABSINTHE:

Brew this aphrodisiac into a tea and drink to increase sexual awareness and potency.

ACACIA:

Burn Acacia powder on charcoal, or mix it with any other gum incense to enhance psychic power.

Burn to please all good spirits and to purify an altar or a ceremonial room.

Some burn it during meditation for protection.

Place this herb over your doorway or bed to keep away evil.

ACACIA

ADAM ROOT:

To be carried by a woman in her pocket, purse, or around her neck to hold the love of her mate.

Can be used in a pair with Eve Root to secure a relationship.

Carry one male (Adam Root) and one female root (Eve Root) in a yellow flannel bag. Add Attraction powder, a Seal of Love *(from the 6th & 7th Books of Moses)* to attract love. If you already have a lover add their picture to the bag to increase love.

ADDERS TONGUE POWDER:

Wrap a picture of San Ramon, Adders Tongue Powder and Stop Gossip Powder in a piece of tin foil. Carry it with you to quiet the tongues of those gossiping about you.

AFRICAN BIRD PEPPER:

Throw this herb in a person's yard to cause him or her problems.

AFRICAN GINGER:

If you suspect that a hex or spell has been cast upon you, sprinkle this herb in each room of your home to cancel negative effects.

Keep African Ginger in jars in your home to stop hexes.

Sprinkle in your yard to stop people from causing you trouble.

Chew to cure a sore throat.

AGAR AGAR:

To bring success when playing bingo, first wash your hands with Siete Machos Soap, then rub your hands with a mixture of Agar Agar and Fast Luck Powder before you play.

AGRIMONY POWDER:

Rub this powder onto a White Image candle or jumbo candle. Burn one inch each day to break any spells or hex that has been placed on you.

Burn as an incense to reverse a spell or hex cast upon you.

ADDERS TONGUE

AGUE:

Put Ague in a Red flannel bag, anoint the bag with Protection Oil and wear on a string around your neck to keep away any negative intent.

To keep evil away from your house, spread this herb around the foundation.

AJENJIBLE:

To make someone move out of your house, add the tea made from this herb to wash water used for his/her clothes.

ALFALFA HERB:

To protect yourself from poverty mix Alfalfa with Money Drawing incense, and burn in your home.

ALFALFA SEED:

Carry a packet containing these seeds in your purse or wallet and your money will go further.

ALLSPICE

ALL HEAL:

When someone is sick make a tea from this herb and sprinkle around the sick room, or bathe the person with the tea mixture.

ALLSPICE:

To attract luck burn this herb with Good Luck Incense every day.

To attract success and prosperity, mix Allspice with Gloria Incense and burn everyday.

ALOE:

If your loved one is away burn this herb with incense every day to keep protect that person and to bring him/her back safely.

Mix with Copal and burn to bring love.

Hang over your front door or in your windows to bring good luck.

ALTHEA:

To pull good spirits to you, keep a jar on the table where you perform your spells, or burn on a white candle.

AMOLE:

Bury in the four corners of your yard for protection.

ANGELICA

ANGELICA:

Sprinkle in the four corners of your house, at the entryways and on the window panes to ward off evil.

Add to your bath to remove any hexes or curses that have been placed on you.

It is said that smoking Angelica Leaves can bring on visions of the future.

Brew Angelica into a tea and drink for relief of indigestion or to help cure a cold.

ANISE ESTRELLA:

Brew into a tea and take a bath to bring your love back, also can be burnt as an incense.

ANISE SEED:

Mix with Camphor and burn, to help make you more clairvoyant or to improve your psychic abilities.

ALOE

APACHE PLUME:

Mix with Bay Leaves and Ash Leaves, make into a tea and wash the wood work and floors in your home to remove a jinx, or to remove negative vibrations people have left in your home.

ARCHANGEL:

To find courage and alleviate fear, carry this herb in a White flannel bag along with a St. Michael holy card.

Burn this herb on charcoal and toss the ashes in the wind in order to force a loved one to come back, or notice you.

ARROWROOT:

Mix with Gambling Powder and rub on your hands before you go gamble.

When playing the lottery, wrap your tickets in a Green cloth along with Lucky Lottery powder, lay it beside a Green Skull candle and burn a little each day.

ANISE

ARTHRITIS ROOT:

To send all kinds of bad luck to an enemy, mix this root with chicken feathers and Powder of Tripas del Diablo. Lay this mixture on a piece of tin foil and let the wax of a black candle drip on it. Fold it all up and throw or place in your enemies yard, car, or house.

ASAFOETIDA POWDER:

If you want to get even with someone by returning misery or distress, sprinkle some of this powder on their front doorstep.

This horrible smelling herb can also be found in chunks. Throw some in a person's car if they've harmed you, they will surely be sorry.

ASAFOETIDA ROOT

Burn this root to hex an enemy or force him to leave you alone. Write your plan on a piece of parchment, place the burnt ash on it and seal it with the wax of a black candle then bury it on the person's property.

ASH LEAVES:

To keep others from making a pass at your lover, place a picture of him or her along with a picture of yourself in a yellow flannel bag along with the Ash Leaves. Carry the bag with you at all times.

AXCOPAQUE

If you have had a sickness in your house, burn this as an incense.

Brew this herb as a tea and sprinkle to cleanse a room from the bad vibes of an illness.

B

BALM:

In the old days Balm would be brewed into a strong tea and then used as a rinse for the entire body to bring new life and tone to a person's skin.

BALM OF GILEAD:

In a red flannel pouch, mix this herb with Rosebuds, Lavendar flowers and Couch Grass. Tie the pouch tightly and wear it on a string around your neck to mend a broken heart and attract a new lover.

Add this herb to your protection bag or mojo bag for good luck while gambling. Protect yourself from the evil eye.

BALMONY:

To cast a potent hex on your enemy, write his / her name on parchment and wrap the parchment in a bundle of Balmony. Burn the bundle with any hexing incense, call out the name of the person being hexed as you light it.

BALMONY ROOT

A powerful hexing root which is ground up and mixed in numerous incense recipes.

BARB DE ELOTE:

Make into a tea, then sprinkle in your yard or garden. It is said to bring good crops or only good people to your home.

BARBERRY.

If you want to protect your home or business from enemies, put this across your path or walkway into your house, or business.

BARBERRY

BARLEY

Scatter this grain on the ground outside around your home or business to keep away evil and negativity.

BASIL:

To enhance your lovelife, sprinkle on your lovers food.

Sprinkle Basil in the bath for a new refreshing love to come into your life, or to wash an old love out of your life.

BASIL

No evil can stay where Basil is placed. If you suspect there is an evil prescence in your home or business spread Basil on the floor throughout the premises.

In a red flannel pouch, mix this herb with Rosebuds, Lavendar Flowers and Couch Grass. Tie the pouch tightly and wear on a string around your neck to mend a broken heart and attract a new lover.

BASIL LEAVES

Dry and crush, then cook into a your food for luck and success.

Dry and crush. It is said that if you cook

BARLEY

Basil into a woman's food it will increase her fertility.

Carry in a red conjure bag around your neck for protection.

BAY

Burn Bay Leaves with Sandalwood Incense to break hexes and ward off evil spirits.

Burn bay leaves with Vision incense to induce prophetic dreams.

BAYBERRY:

Burn a White candle in a glass and sprinkle Bayberry in it; as it burns it attracts money and good fortune.

Keep this herb somewhere on your person to attract financial gain and good luck in all endeavors.

BAY

BAY LEAVES:

Bay is the best herb for protection. It can be placed in the home or business. Once a week, sprinkle the leaves on the floor throughout the premises, and then sweep out through the front door.

BENZOIN:

Burn with Cinnamon and Copal for better business.

Burn Benzoin to protect and cleanse a home before moving in.

BERGAMOT

BERGAMOT:

Burning this herb during any magical ritual will add power and better your chances for success.

BETHEL NUT:

Carry for good luck and protection.

BETHEL ROOT

If you wish to increase your lover's desire for you, grind this root into a powder and add it to his / her food.

BERGAMOT

Carry with a Cross of Caravaca in a Blue bag for good luck in gambling.

To increase clairvoyant powers chew this root thoroughly.

BETONY:

Burn as a incense, do a smudge cleansing, as the incense is burning rub the smoke on your body, or make a strong tea and after you bathe pour it over your head.

BISTORT:

Burn with Frankincense for luck in a hurry.

Carry it with you for good fortune.

BETHEL TREE /
BETHEL NUT

BITTERSWEET:

This is a hexing herb. Mix with Bitter root, Hexing powder and Black salt, then throw in the path of your enemy.

BLACKBERRY:

This is a sacred herb. It should be used to remove evil spirits, demons or any other types of evil.

For returning evil back to a person doing you harm, carve the name of your target into a Black Image candle. Place the candle on a piece of red cloth, pour some Black Salt over it and wrap it up with some Blackberry leaves then tie it with Black ribbon. Hit it with a hammer a couple of times. Call out the person's name and what you want to return back to the person. Then every couple of days hit it with the hammer again repeating what you said, then throw it in a deep hole.

BLACK COHOSH

BLACK COHOSH:

To use this herb for protection make it into a tea and bathe in it.

Brew into a potent tea and sprinkle all around a room to eliminate evil spirits.

To improve your love life cook this herb into a meal.

If you are weak, afraid, timid, or shy, brew this herb into a tea and bathe in it everyday, also use Siete Machos Soap.

BLACK MUSTARD SEED:

To cause trouble to a person mix Black Mustard seed with Hexing Powder and leave in a person's house or throw it in their doorway.

BLADDER WRACK:

Make into a tea and mop the floors, wash the windows and sprinkle in the door way of a business to attract customers.

Very strong for people who like to fish, take a bath in this tea before going fishing, and soak the hooks in this mixture.

BLOOD ROOT:

Burn or carry a piece in a red flannel bag to defeat hexes.

To keep away evil, blend thoroughly with Blue Stone, Sugar and Cinnamon. Wrap in a piece of red flannel and carry it with you.

Burn as a incense or carry the root if someone is trying to take your husband or lover.

Sew some into your mates pillow to help keep them faithful.

Keep this root with you to attract a new lover.

BLOODROOT

BLUEBERRY LEAVES:

Put a cup of the leaves into a bowl of hot water, sprinkle some Black Mustard seeds on top and cover the bowl with tin foil. Let it soak overnight. On the following day throw in your enemy's path. It is said this will make them feel sad and blue.

BLUE FLAG

BLUE COHOSH:

If someone has jinxed your car, wash it thoroughly, then make a tea of Blue Cohosh in a gallon of water and rinse the car to wash the evil away.

BLUE FLAG:

A very expensive herb, but it is one of the best money drawing herbs. Mix it with money drawing incense and burn once a week or everyday for quick money drawing.

Keep some in the cash box or register to draw more money.

Carry some in a green flannel bag so you will never run out of money.

BOLDO

BOLDO LEAVES:

Sprinkle around the home to remove any type of evil.

BONESET:

This herb is very good for exorcisms, rub the leaves on the body of the possessed and then burn them outside.

BORAGE

BORAGE:

When you want peace in the home, make this herb into a tea and sprinkle around the house.

Carry this herb with you to increase courage and confidence in any situation. It is also said to enhance perceptive abilities.

BROOM TOPS:

Make into a tea and sprinkle inside and outside your home to keep evil out.

Very good for cleansing, put in a cloth and rub on the body everyday.

Brew into a tea and sprinkle around in an effort to break a hex and eliminate evil spirits.

BUCKEYE ROOT

Keep this root well wrapped in red flannel and carry it with you to bring success in any undertaking.

BUCKTHORN

BUCKTHORN

To have one wish granted, brew into a strong tea and sprinkle in a small circle during a full moon. Dance inside the circle and concentrate on your desire.

BUCHU:

Mix with Frankincense and burn as incense to help have prophetic dreams.

Readers should keep Buchu near their reading area, as it helps them tell the future.

BURDOCK

BURDOCK:

Boil in water and let cool. Use as a floor wash for purifying areas were rituals are to be held. Sprinkle in all four corners of the room during ritual.

Carry in a white flannel bag for protection.

Add to mojo bags for extra strength.

BUTTON ROOT

To protect your premises from undesirables, place this root outside your front door underneath your welcome mat.

Add power to any hexing, controlling or dominating spell. Soak in salty water for nine days then use to sprinkle around an altar to during the ritual.

C

CACTUS

Keep burgulars out of your home by placing a cactus near each window or entry way.

Protect your property by placing a Cactus at each point of the compass.

Finally, a Cactus draws negative energy to it so the energy does not come to you.

CACTUS

CACTUS FLOWER:

To keep evil, harm and witchcraft from your home or place or business, place the following items in a pint jar: nails, needles, lodestones, Cactus Flower, Ruda, Rosemary and Mace, then bury it by your front door.

CACTUS THORNS:

Used to mark names and signs on candles, roots, or to write in ink on parchment paper.

Cactus thorns are a most powerful tool for sticking voodoo dools.

CALAMUS:

A powerful controlling root. It is popular in Voodoo because of its strength. Add power to any hexing, controlling or dominating spell by burning as an incense during rituals.

Simply growing this plant brings luck to the gardener.

CAMPHOR

CALENDULA FLOWERS:

To protect against nightmares and make certain all dreams come true, sprinkle dried bits of this flower under your bed.

CAMPHOR:

Burn a mixture of Camphor and Dream Incense in your bedroom. Burn it before going to bed burn to help you have prophetic dreams.

Place Camphor blocks in the corners of your rooms to ward off evil.

CARAWAY

CARAWAY SEEDS:

To protect against illness, harm or hexes of any kind place these seeds along with some Rosemary in a red flannel bag, anoint it with Patchouly Oil and carry it with you every day.

CATNIP

CASCARA SAGRADA:

Make an infusion of this herb and sprinkle around your house before going to court, to receive a favorable verdict.

To have the judge look upon your evidence favorably, place this herb along with Success Powder in the briefcase containing your court papers.

To help win court cases, brew into a potent tea and sprinkle around the court room.

CAYENNE

CATNIP:

Add to love potions, to calm down a rocky relationship.

Mix with Rose Petals in a love sachet to spice up your relationship.

Brew into a tea sweeten with pure honey and drink. It will calm your nerves and break even the most powerful spell.

CAYENNE POWDER:

Very powerful effect when added to any jinxing or separation spells.

CEDAR

A piece of Cedar wrapped in with your roll of dollar bills *(any denomination)* attracts more money.

CELANDINE

To attract customers to your business mix Cedar with Better Business Incense and burn all day at the entrance to your establishment.   *(continued)*

When burned as an incense the scent can help alleviate the symptoms of a head cold.

CELANDINE:

To keep the law away, spread one pound of Celandine all around your yard at midnight.

CELERY SEED:

Burn with Orris Root as an incense to help bring on deep concentration and prophecies.

CELERY

CENIZO:

This herb is used when you want to hold on to your money. Put your money in a jar of Cenizo, and leave it there over night.

To give you that extra luck brew a tea of Cenizo and wash your hands in it before picking your lottery numbers, playing cards, rolling dice or gambling money in any way.

CHAMOMILE:

Protect your children from any kind of harm by making this herb into a tea and adding it to your child's bath water.

If you are trying to get your mate to propose mix this herb with Marriage Oil and sprinkle onto the sheets of your bed prior to making love.

CHAMOMILE

Brew and use as a hand wash before playing cards or gambling. It is said to insure luck and constant winning if used with regularity.

CHERRY BARK:

Wrap a picture of your lover in a red cloth along with Cherry Bark to make him more passionate.

If your lover has left you and you wish to spoil his chances with another, wrap his/her picture in a Black cloth along Cherry Bark and burn it in a hot flaming fire, his nature will leave him when he is with someone else.

CHEWING JOHN ROOT :

To reverse the effect of a hex and cause harm to the one who cursed you in the first place, chew on a piece of the root, while concentrating on your wish or desire, then spit it out.

CHICKWEED

To attract a new romance or maintain a relationship mix Chick Weed, Roses, Damiana and Orange Blossoms into your bath water.

To maintain a good marriage add a little bit to each partners food everyday.

Bring peace to your home by sprinkling tea brewed from this herb throughout the house.

CHICORY

CHICORY ROOT

To curse an enemy, write your intent on parchment in black ink and fold it in a way that you can sprinkle in powdered Chicory root. Seal it with the wax of a black candle and bury it in the yard of your nemesis. Said to work without fail.

(continued)

Sprinkle Chicory and Cayenne powder on a picture of your enemy and fold it. For the next three days, at least once a day, stomp on it while wishing the bastard bad luck, then throw it in a hole. Your enemies fortunes will surely follow.

CINNAMON

CHILI PEPPER:

To make an existing love affair more passionate rub this powder into any paper or card and write your partner a love letter on it.

CINCHONA:

To increase your chances of winning when playing bingo or at the race track, carry this herb in a yellow bag along with some Tonka Beans. Anoint the bag with Lucky Gambler's oil. Wipe your cards or tickets with the bag to remove any bad vibes.

CINNAMON:

For the strongest protection from evil intentions aimed at you or your home, mix with Frankincense, Myrrh, and Sandalwood powder and burn each day.

Burn the incense formulated above before you start any spell or ritual to cleanse the room. When you are finished doing the spell to protect you, let the smoke drift over your nude body and feel the good vibrations.

Brewed in a tea Cinnamon is especially good for relief of colds & diarrhea.

CINQUEFOIL

For protection in any situation, mix powdered Cinnamon with baby powder and apply to your body before going out.

CINQUEFOIL:

CLOVE

A powerful money drawing effect can be established by mixing Cinquefoil, Cinnamon, Cloves, and 4 Tonka Beans in a green flannel bag. Carry the bag with you at all times. Anoint the bag with Money Drawing oil while saying a money drawing prayer each day.

CLOVE:

Burn Clove powder as an incense to attract good luck to your home.

Chewing on a piece of Clove while thinking of a lover is said to make them do your every bidding.

Rub Clove into a Green candle and burn it to attract wealth.

To stop gossip and remove negative vibrations burn Clove as an incense while burning a red candle.

COLTSFOOT

CLOVER (FOUR LEAF):

Carry in your wallet for extreme luck and to make your money multiply.

CLOVER (RED):

Keep away evil by adding an infusion of the plant to your bath water.

COFFEE BEAN HUSK:

One of the best herbs to bathe in to remove a jinx, it is very powerful.

COLIC ROOT:

Brew into a tea and sprinkle around the home to stop strife and arguments.

COLTSFOOT:

Burn the leaves to help you see the future.

COMFREY:

To make a business trip profitable, brew Comfrey into a tea and sprinkle it on your luggage before departure.

Good for mojo and good luck bags.

Rub some on your money to help you hold on to it.

COMFREY

CONTRA YERBA:

Excellent for protection. Carry 3 pieces in your pocket in a Green flannel bag to keep all evil, jinxes and the evil eye away.

COPAL:

This is a resin incense, that is burned in the home to remove evil and bless the house. Pray psalm 23 aloud while this is burning in your home.

CORIANDER

CORIANDER:

Add to love spells to draw love to you. Carry some of the seeds in a Yellow flannel bag with the name of the person you wish to attract.

Blend with a little of your favorite wine for a splendid aphrodisiac.

CORN FLOWERS:

Brew into a tea, sprinkle inside and outside the house to bring peace and happiness to a marriage.

COWSLIP:

Sprinkle in your front yard and leave on your porch if you don't want any visitors.

CONTRA YERBA

CRUEL MAN OF THE WOODS:

Use to return evil to the sender. Write the persons name on a Black candle, then roll the candle in this herb. Burn the candle for 5 minutes a day. When it is all consumed, throw the remains into a hole, and cover the hole with salt.

CUBEB BERRIES:

Known as the love berry. Use in your bath water or carry in a Red flannel bag.

Makes a lover more amorous or a prospective lover more willing. Must be powdered and then eaten by the one you desire.

CORNFLOWER

CUMIN SEED:

Mix Cumin seed with Witch Salt and sprinkle around your home or business to keep away evil spirits and bad luck.

Soak Cumin seeds in Peace Water for nine days and then sprinkle in every corner of the house. Said to create harmony and bring peace of mind to all living there.

CURRY:

Burn during jinx removing and reversing rituals to add more power in difficult cases.

D

DAMIANA:

First, allow the herb to dry then ground it into a powder and add it to coffee, tea or wine. It is *the* love herb a potent aphrodisiac. Makes men ready and increases their nature.

Also use in a love bath.

DANDELION:

Sew tightly in a red flannel bag and wear around the neck to make wishes come true.

Brew into a tea and drink to induce clairvoyance.

DEVIL BONE:

Bring harm to your enemy with the following ritual. Write your enemies name on a Black Candle, then anoint the candle with Devil Oil, then roll the candle in Devil Bone. Burn the candle on the night of the full moon, while the candle is burning say aloud your request.

DEVIL'S CLAW

If someone has you trapped, and has you blocked, boil one half pound of Devil's Claw, and everyday after bathing, pour it over your body and say the following:

"Devil take your claws from my life and return to where you came from."

Do this for 7 days, wear Protection powder daily.

DEVIL"S DUNG:

If a person has done you wrong, throw this herb in his yard, car, or place of business. Make sure you wash your hands with Florida Water after you touch it.

DEVIL'S SHOESTRING:

Carry this root in a White flannel bag with some Protection powder for protection against evil, harm or gossip.

Carry in a Green flannel bag for good luck.

Cut up fine. Add whiskey and camphor. Rub this mixture on your hands. It is said to give a man total power over the woman he desires, or a woman can gain control over a specific man.

To bring back a lover, take some dirt from his left footprint along his path. Add some Devil's Shoestring and place this in one of his socks or her stocking. Then place it into your closet.

Write your desire in Dove's Blood Ink on pure parchment. Wrap this root in the parchment and anoint it each day with Attraction oil and carry it with you.

A piece of this root carried in the pocket at all times will bring luck to gamblers.

Placed in the path of an enemy, he or she will have to face financial ruin.

For help with court cases, carry this herb wrapped in parchment paper. On the paper, in Dove's Blood ink, or red ink, write what you need done. Anoint it with Just Judge oil and carry it with you in court.

DIABETINA:

Carry some in a Blue flannel bag along with a piece of coral, and a crystal to help ward off illnesses.

DILL

Add to hot wine and serve. Increases passion of those who drink it. An aphrodisiac that is said to never fail a Voodoo practitioner.

DILL SEED:

Good for love. To help you get the person you desire place the following items in a Red flannel bag and carry it with you. Dill seed, a pair of red lodestones, one needle.

DILL WEED:

This is for a man or woman when you are crossed or jinxed in a love affair. Make an infusion of this herb , while it is

brewing add a pinch of Ginger Root to the water. After you have taken a bath rub this tea over your body, be sure you rub all parts, let it dry on your body. Do this for 9 days using a new batch of tea everyday. Good for men who have had their nature taken away.

DITTANY OF CRETE:

Is an old and famous herb. Said to be good for love spells.

Burn as an incense for astral projection, mix with Vanillan powder, Benzoin, Sandalwood and burn on charcoal in the same room you are traveling. Burn every night until you reach your goal.

DOG ROSE:

Carry in a Red flannel bag mixed with Chia Seeds to ward off curses or jinx.

DRAGON'S BLOOD CHUNKS:

A chunk of Dragon's Blood carried in a Red flannel bag is the best charm to attract good luck, add a piece of Alum rock for added strength.

DRAGONS BLOOD POWDER:

Burn in the home to evacuate evil spirits. This is good to burn when you are moving into a new home to cleanse the premises.

DULSE:

Bring peace and tranquility back into a troubled home by sprinkling this herb throughout the premises.

E

EARTH SMOKE:

For quick money gain, make into a tea and sprinkle inside and outside the business or residence. If you are a sales man, put some on the bottom of your shoes. *(Also called Fumitory)*

ELCAMPANE

ECHINACEA:

Used by the indians as an offering to the spirits when seeking aid from them.

ELDER:

Put some in a White flannel bag and hang above your front and back door for protection from witchcraft, hexing and brujeria.

ELDER FLOWERS:

Protects a home from attack when dried and sprinkled into each corner.

EUCALYPTUS

ELECAMPANE:

Mix with Vervain and Mistletoe in a Pink flannel bag and carry it with you to attract love. A true love powder.

EUCALYPTUS:

Use to stuff Voodoo dolls or use in a cleansing bath.

To relieve the symptoms of a cold, brew this leaf into a tea (do not drink). Breathe the vapor as it rises.

EVE ROOT:

To be carried by a man in his pocket, wallet, or around his neck to hold the love of his mate. Can be used in a pair with an Adam Root to hold a relationship together.

EYEBRIGHT:

Burn in a bedroom before going to sleep. Makes all dreams come true in seven days.

EYEBRIGHT

F

FENNEl

FENNEL:

Carry for protection, helps keep the law away. Carry some of the seeds along with 3 Law Stay Away chips, in a Blue flannel bag, anoint daily with law stay away oil.

Brew into a strong tea and drink while warm. Best when added to wine and utilized as an aphrodisiac. Popular with Voodooists today.

Sprinkle ground Fennel into your food to relieve a nervous or gaseous stomach.

FENUGREEK:

Add the seeds to your mop water to help bring money into the home.

Carry the seeds in your purse to help attract riches.

FERN:

Burn on charcoal, to remove evil spirits from the home.

Mix with Bay Leaves and keep by the front door to help ward off burglars.

FENUGREEK

FEVERFEW:

For accident prone people. Carry some in your pocket.

FIVE FINGER GRASS:

To remove stubborn curses that have been placed on you. Take a bath in this tea for 9 days.

FIVE FINGER ROOT:

Add to mojo bags and charm bags for gambling luck.

FLAX

To attract money, place a few Flax Seeds in your wallet and keep it with you.

It is said that a few of these seeds placed in your shoes will keep you from going broke.

FLAX

Drink a tea brewed with Flax Seeds to enhance your psychic visions. Scatter the seeds on the floor of your spiritual room to increase your mental powers.

FENUGREEK

FLOR AZAHAR:

Take a bath in these flowers. to help bring on a proposal of marriage.

FRANKINCENSE:

A most powerful mystical incense. Add to any ritual to increase the power. It is one of the three Holy incense.

Combine it with sandalwood, and myrrh and it can be used everyday as a general purpose incense.

GALANGAL

G

GALANGAL ROOT:

Soak the root in sugared water and chew for protection or to bring money.

Carry in your pocket for success in court cases.

GARLIC:

Burn as an incense with Bay Leaves to remove any type of evil.

Add to mop water or cleansing water to remove evil.

GENTIAN:

Brings love. Put in your bath water, and carry some in a Red bag along with the name of the person you want.

Brew into a tea and bottle while still hot. Then add a tablespoon to your bath water. Said to attract many new friends, perhaps even a lover.

Add to your bath or use in a love sachet.

GENTIAN

GINGER:

Used very often in love spells to enhance their power and bring quicker results. It can be added to food or burned with incense.

GOATS RUE:

Carry to protect yourself from sudden death.

GOLDEN SEAL:

Mix with healing incense for better health.

Brew into a tea and sprinkle in each corner of your business establishment. It helps increase profits and brings people to your door.

GINGER

To attract abundance and wealth, burn this herb with Money Drawing incense and at the same time you can burn a Gold candle anointed with Goldenseal oil.

GOLONDRINA:

Soak your feet in this tea, when you feel you have stepped on something evil and your feet burn.

GOTA KOLA:

Mix with Mediation incense.

GRAINS OF PARADISE:

GRAINS OF PARADISE

Put a picture of St. Michael at the front door and back door, place a bag of this herb behind each picture for protection of the home and family.

A sexual stimulant. Must be added to food. One of the best known Voodoo aphrodisiacs.

Carry the grains in a Green mojo bag to bring luck.

GRAVEL ROOT:

Said to help those seeking employment. Bathe in this tea before going to look for a job. Carry in a Red flannel bag when going on your interview.

GROUND IVY:

GOLDENSEAL

Burn with Hexing incense to cast a spell against someone you dislike.

GUINEA PEPPER:

To cause harm to an enemy, lay out a black cloth, place on the cloth a rabbit's foot, Black Peppercorns, graveyard dirt, and Guinea Pepper, write the enemies name on sheepskin parchment paper. Wrap the cloth and tie with a black ribbon and place it near or in your enemies house, car, or place of business. Your enemy will slowly become weaker.

To cause harm to an enemy. Fill a 1 pint jar with Guinea Pepper, Four Thieves Vinegar, a Wolf Heart and your enemies name written on parchment paper with Dragon's Blood ink. Every night for 13 nights at the same time burn a Black candle on the lid of the jar and curse your foe with the following:

"(Name of your enemy), I curse thee. May your money go away. May your mind wander. May your family go away and leave you in loneliness. May your heart wither of jealousy."

On the 13th night bury the jar in an old cemetery. Now go home and light 13 White candles that have been rubbed with Protection oil.

H

HARDY YELLOW TRUMPET:

Use in your bath on the night of the full moon to help attract a new lover by the new moon.

HAWTHORN BERRIES:

When someone is trying to steal your mate, put this in their path to stop them.

HEAL ALL HERB:

Use in bath for gambling luck.

HEARTEASE:

Bathe in this after a break up of a relationship, to help get over the pain faster.

HIBISCUS:

Can be used with Love incense, or carried for love drawing. Carry in a Red bag with the picture of the person you want.

HIGH JOHN THE CONQUEROR ROOT:

The most famous of all Voodoo roots. Carry with you at all timeses to help remove and conquer all obstacles in your path.

Carry in a green bag for good luck, money drawing and power over others. Anoint daily with John the Conqueror Oil.

Attract a specific lover by carrying this root and a lock of hair from the one you desire in a Red chamois bag anointed with Attraction Oil.

A fantastic good luck charm when kept in your pocket while gambling.

Carry in your pocket to offset moods of depression and confusion.

HOLY GHOST:

Drink this to remove evil from the body.

HOLY THISTLE:

Make into a tea and sprinkle all around the outside of the house to defeat all curses.

This herb is very helpful in any hex breaking ritual.

HOREHOUND

HOPS:

Stuff a pillow with Hops to help ward off nightmares and ensure a sound and peaceful slumber.

HOREHOUND:

Carry in a white flannel bag to ward off jealous and envious people.

HOREHOUND LEAVES

Dry and pulverize then add to a bowl of water and place by a sick person's bed. Said to heal.

HUCKLEBERRY

HORSETAIL:

Keep under an infants crib or bed for protection against harm, evil and the evil eye.

HUCKLEBERRY

Placed in a Red flannel bag and carried with you these leaves are said to bring good luck.

Helps overcome despair. Simply boil in rainwater and sprinkle around the room.

HYDRANGEA ROOT:

Mix with incense and burn. Used to help get a loved one released from jail.

HYSSOP:

All participants in any ritual ceremony should add this tea to their bathwater to purify, cleanse and remove all negativity prior to beginning work.

ICELAND MOSS

I

ICELAND MOSS

Sprinkle this herb in the path of your enemy to return any evil intent.

INDIAN TOBACCO

Burn this herb in your home to bring peace and calm when family members are bickering.

IRISH MOSS:

Place in your place of business under a rug and carry in the pocket to increase a steady, flow of money.

Stuff into Green voodoo dolls for to draw money and bring good luck when gambling.

HORSETAIL

J

JABORANDI:

Alleged to help make your hair grow. Make into a strong tea and rinse your scalp with it.

JAMAICA GINGER:

Place in a Red flannel bag and carry while gambling for good luck. It is said to guarantee big winnings.

JASMINE:

Said to be a powerful aid in love spells. Can be burned as an incense.

Mix with Orris Root and Rose Petals for a very potent love bath.

JASMINE

Mix with Lovers Incense and burn along with a Pink Candle to attract a lover or make a relationship stronger.

JERSEY TEA:

Indians would rub this on their body before bathing for 8 days to remove evil or jinx.

JEZEBEL ROOT:

A powerful money herb. Burn a Green candle anointed with Jezebel oil. Gather the wax and mold it into a ball. Push a Jezebel Root and a penny into the ball,

JUNIPER

sprinkle Money Drawing powder on it and then bury it at a crossroad. You will soon have a boost in your income.

To break up a couple, rub your hands with Controlling oil. Hold a Jezebel Root in your left hand and a Black Candle anointed with Break Up oil in your right hand. Concentrate deeply on the couple and see them splitting. Burn the Black candle and as the wax drips, gather it to mold around the root. Bury the root in your back yard and your job is done.

JOB TEARS:

Carry seven Job Tears with a Cross of Caravaca talisman and anoint with Hi John Conqueror Oil for good luck in any type of gambling.

JOE PIE:

Carry in Blue flannel bag and add some Attraction Powder for popularity and friendship. If there are a few people who you specifically have in mind add their pictures to the bag.

JUNIPER:

Use this herb in a hot bath, inhale the steam for relief from a cold or respiratory infection.

JOHNNY JUMPER:

Used by men when they want a lot of sexual activity. Carry in Blue flannel bag, mixed with 4 Tonka Beans and anoint it with Irresistable Oil.

JUNIPER BERRIES:

Add to wine and let sit for three weeks before drinking. Take daily doses for sexual potency.

K

KAVA KAVA:

It is said that drinking a tea brewed from this root will stimulate your sex life.

Add 2 ounces to 2 quarts of water, then add Good Luck Lotion and let sit overnight. Use one cup a day in your bath water to attract good luck and love.

KELP

Use as a floor wash to increase business and to bring general good luck in all affairs.

KHUS KHUS:

Carry in Red flannel bag for good luck in business or when going to look for a job.

Add to bath water and it will make you irresistable to the opposite sex.

KING OF THE WOODS:

This herb was used in the old days by male witches to seduce young virgins.

Used by men to control women and to make you desirable to the opposite sex. Carry in a Yellow flannel bag a piece of Low John the Conqueror Root.

KNOT GRASS

Use for casting extremely evil spells on an enemy who has really caused you harm. Use only at night and only with a black candle.

KNOTWEED

KNOTWEED:

To bind two lovers together, or to make your marriage stronger. Take a clean red cloth and lay it on the table, put your lover's picture face to face with your own. Cover the pictures with 2 ounces of Knotweed and Controlling Powder. Fold the cloth around the pictures and tie with a 2 shoelaces, one from each partner's shoe, Anoint weekly with Binding Oil and keep it under your bed.

To bind your enemy or stop his luck. Take a black cloth, one ounce of Knotweed, one Devil Shoestring, and the name or picture of your enemy. Add Controlling powder and Hexing oil. Tie the bundle with black ribbon and put it in a shoe box and everyday step on the bundle and say:

> "(Name of enemy) may your luck go away. May your good fortune go away."

On the fourth day throw the bundle into the river or bury in a hole.

L

LADIES THUMB :

Take an 8 inch piece of tin foil and lay it flat. On it, place the picture of the one you want; along with Love Drawing powder and Rose petals. Fold and seal with the wax from a red candle then bury it by your front door.

LADIES SLIPPER:

Ladies wear this in their left shoe to attract potential sexual encounters.

LAVENDER:

Mix with Rose Petals and Orange Flowers for a love drawing, relaxation and tranquility bath.

LAVENDAR

In a red pouch, carry the following: Lavender, 2 Tonka beans, a Vanilla bean, Rosebuds, Vervain and Couch Grass. Concentrate on what you want as you mix these, then add a little Attraction Powder.

To attract luck with finance, place this herb in a green pouch. Add a penny, a nickel, a quarter and a dollar bill. Carry it with you and the money will multiply.

LEMON GRASS:

For a potentially wild sexual encounter, make an infusion of Lemon Grass, and rub on your private parts before going out.

LEMON

LEMON

For a good outcome to a court proceeding, cut a lemon in half, put salt on one half and wrap it in a new linen handkerchief. Do the same with the other half. Put one in your pocket or purse. Before going into the courtroom, rub one of the lemon halves briskly on your hands, towards you. When you enter the court, take the other half and squirt the juice into your hand. Read Psalm 23; this will help win your case.

LICORICE:

Used to gain power over others. Use a piece of tin foil 8 inch square and on top of it put one ounce of licorice and some Controlling powder, write the person's name on a piece of parchment paper 7 times with Doves Blood Ink. Fold the tin foil and bury on persons property or near their place of employment.

LIGNUM ALOES:

Use for blessing the room where rituals or spells are performed.

Use as an incense to get rid of fear and evil spirits.

LILY

LIFE EVERLASTING

This is a potent charm against diseases and even minor illnesses. Said to prolong life when brewed as a tea and sipped with meals.

LILY

If you want to break a love spell that you think has been cast on you, Carry a fresh lily.

LINDEN FLOWERS

Grind fine and make into a moist paste. Rub on your heart each evening before going to bed. It is said to keep a lover true to you always.

LINSEED:

Take a piece of parchment paper 8 x 11 and draw a cross with glue, then sprinkle Linseed on the glue, which should then form a cross. Hang over doors to keep all evil out and protect the home from being burglarized.

LINDEN

LOTUS:

Burn a Lotus pod with any drawing incense to increase its magnetic powers.

LOVAGE:

Make a potent tea of this root and pour into your bath water just prior to your court proceeding.

Place in your bathwater for ten minutes before you bathe. Said to make you more dynamic by increasing your natural physical magnetism.

LINSEED

6 days prior to appearing in court place Lovage Root and two quarts of water into a jar. Place your court papers under the jar for 3 days. Pour part of this water into your bath each day for three days preceeding your scheduled date, you should receive the outcome you're hoping for.

LOW JOHN THE CONQUEROR ROOT:

Use an infusion of this root in your bath water to remove hexes or curses.

When chewing the root spit behind your enemy to pacify them.

LUNGWORT

For help in all love situations, cook this herb into your lover's meal.

LUNGWORT

M

MACE:

In the old days this was a very powerful love herb. Women mixed a pinch of this with vinegar and used it as a love douche. Once she took the man to bed he was in her control.

MAGNOLIA ROOT

Place under a mattress or on the floor under a bed. Overcomes frigidity in sexual love and makes your love partner faithful.

MAIDENHAIR FERN:

MAIDENHAIR

In ancient times this herb was used to bring beauty and love into your life. Use 1 ounce a day for a love bath. Also carry it in your purse.

(continued)

Immerse Maiden Hair in a glass of water and let soak overnight. Use this water as a hand and face wash before going out for the evening to attract a new relationship.

MALE FERN:

To attract the love of a man, put his name in an envelope with Male Fern and carry it in your purse.

MANDRAKE:

A famous magical root. At one time you could buy pieces that looked like a male or female, but people today buy pieces and glue them together in the shape of a woman or man. To get the lover you want, glue the root into the shape of the man or woman desired. Write that person's name on parchment paper, wrap it around the figure and anoint with Mandrake oil. Wrap it in a clean cloth and put it under your pillow.

MANDRAKE ROOT

You can purchase a bottle of oil with Mandrake root in it. Add to it one silver dime. Use this to draw money, also rub on your money and wallet

Take a Mandrake root and carve the name of the person you want into the root. As you do this, tell it what you want to be done. Add Red Clover, Rose and a piece of Willow. Wrap all the ingredients in a piece of red satin and place it under your pillow.

When added to food this herb will increase one's sexuality.

Protects a person from all harm when carried in a red flannel sack or chamois bag.

MANZANILLA:

Wash your hands in this tea before going to bingo or for any gambling.

Keep your lottery tickets or betting slips with a pack of Manzanilla.

MARIGOLD:

Put 4 ounces of Marigold under your pillow before going to bed to help you have prophetic dreams.

Add to your bathwater to gain the respect of others and have greater influence on all in your presence. Perfect in business situations.

MARIGOLD

The morning that you go to court, add Marigolds to your bath water to be thought of favorably. Also carry the herb in your pocket when you are in court.

MARJORAM:

Place in each room of the house or business. Protects the home or business from evil influence or jinx. Must be changed once a month to be effective.

Brew into a tea and bathe a person who is sad or grieving for 7 days.

May be placed in the corners of a house to uncross or break hexes.

MARSHMALLOW HERB:

MARJORAM

Brew into a tea and add to your bath water. Protects against all harm. Especially good for protecting little children.

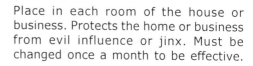

MASTER OF THE WOODS:

A very powerful herb for any situation in which you need control over another person. Simply carrying it with you allows your influence to determine any outcome.

To dominate someone or to have power over them sprinkle this herb in their path or where they are sure to touch it.

Mix with Boss Fix powder and rub on your body before going to ask for a raise.

MAY APPLE

Carry in your pocket to protect against ever going broke.

MAY APPLE

MESQUITE:

When cleansing magical tools or your Voodoo room, burn Mesquite as an incense.

Can also be used as an purification bath.

MISTLETOE:

One of the true love powders. Also a very good love bath. Use for good luck when hunting for a mate.

If your lover has a wandering eye, mix Mistletoe with Commanding Incense and keep your mate from straying.

MISTLETOE

MOTHERWORT:

If your family is in danger, make a strong tea and put in their bath water, also wash the clothes in this mixture. The dog can

MUGWORT

also be washed in this mixture.

Keep some in a jar by the family pictures to keep your loved ones safe.

MUGWORT:

Make this into a mild tea to wash your crystals. This will remove any jinx the crystal has picked up and will add strength to it. Can also be burnt on charcoal before crystal gazing.

Place this herb in your shoes to produce energy and vitality.

Sleep on a pillow stuffed with this herb to produce prophetic dreams.

MULLEIN

MULLIEN:

A tea made from these flowers will help you sleep and reduce minor aches and pains.

Stuff Mullein in your pillow to prevent nightmares.

Very powerful when used as an incense in black magic spells. You can use this herb to substitute for candles in a emergency situation.

If someone lacks courage bathe them in this for 5 days.

Mix with Graveyard Dust to make it more powerful.

MUSTARD SEED

MUSTARD SEED (RED):

Mix with Mistletoe and sprinkle around the house. Especially in the bedroom to protect your lover from others.

MUSTARD SEED (YELLOW):

Mix with Come to Me powder and the name of your lover and carry in a red cloth bag for love.

Mix with Protection powder and sprinkle around the house for protection.

MYRRH:

One of the 3 holy incenses. Myrrh is used to bring peace and for purifying areas. It should be mixed with Frankincense and/or Copal. Myrrh is rarely burnt alone. This incense when used correctly is very effective.

MYRTLE:

A love herb. Add to all love spells and love baths to keep the love alive and sex exciting.

Every bride should carry some Myrtle in her bra when getting married, to insure and long and happy marriage.

Wear to encourage sexuality. Toss pieces of this herb into the path of someone you desire, they will soon be yours alone. Makes one inspiring.

Keep this herb in the corners of your kitchen to protect yourself from hunger and lack of money to buy food.

N

NETTLES:

Excellent for removing a curse. Mix with pure Jinx Removing powder and draw a solid unbroken line across the doorway with the mixture.

NUTMEG:

NETTLES

For a most powerful money drawing lucky charm for gamblers follow these instructions. Bore a hole into the nut. Fill the hole with Quicksilver and seal it with wax from a Green candle. Carry it with 3 silver coins in a red flannel bag when playing games of chance.

Used in many prosperity spells. Can be ground and then sprinkled onto a Green Candle and burned.

Use a piece of parchment paper. Write in Dove's Blood Ink the amount of money you wish to come to you. Wrap the parchment around a whole nutmeg and carry it with your change.

NUTMEG

O

OAK:

The most royal of all trees. Burn Oak and Mistletoe together to remove spirits or ghosts from the house or business.

Also good when mixed in love spells.

ORANGE BLOSSOM

Blend with equal parts of Orris powder and Anise Seed, burn in order to locate a lover or to gain a marriage partner.

ORANGE FLOWERS

ORANGE FLOWERS:

If your hoping for a marriage proposal add Orange Flowers to your bath prior to seeing your lover.

OREGON GRAPE ROOT:

Carry in Green flannel bag with Money Drawing powder to attract money and popularity.

OREGANO:

Sprinkle Oregano and Law Stay Away powder, around your house to keep the law away.

Mix with Stay Away powder and put where the in-laws will touch to keep them away.

ORRIS

ORRIS ROOT

A love root which attracts the opposite sex. Carry in a Red flannel sack, or grind into a fine powder and sprinkle on the clothing of the one you desire.

P

PALO AZUL:

Make into a tea and use to remove any jinx or hex. Sprinkle the tea around your home or use it in your bath. It is very powerful.

PALO SANTO:

When someone has cursed you with the devil or strange things have been happening to you, make an infusion of the herb and use it in your bathwater.

PAPAYA LEAVES:

Mix with a Mandrake root and burn or bathe to protect yourself from a spell, hex, or jinx. After doing so you can then wear Reversible powder for added protection and retaliation.

Place these leaves along with a Mandrake Root in a sachet and hang it in the doorway of your home or business.

PARSLEY:

Mix Parsley with Jasmine and carry in your shoe to make you more attractive to the opposite sex

Brew into a tea and drink to calm your nerves and to bring a turn of good luck.

PASSION FLOWER:

To have luck with love, carry in a Red flannel bag with an Agate stone and anoint the bag with Love Drawing oil.

To protect yourself from an angry individual with hurtful intent, dry and sprinkle Passion Flower in front of your your doors and windows. Stops anger from hurting you.

PATCHOULY:

Known as a love herb, mix with Rose Petals, Orange Flowers, and Orris root for a very superb love bath. Makes you feel real sexy.

This herb is used very often in spells designed to attract money or wealth. It can be sprinkled in your wallet or purse, burned with Money Drawing incense or burned with Green candles.

PATCHOULY LEAVES

Used to break a marriage or an affair. Must be used with Black Image Candles and Black Arts Incense.

PEACH TREE:

Mix the leaves in Concentration oil and Success oil to help pass tests.

PARSLEY

PASSION FLOWER

PEACH TREE

PEPPERMINT

PEPPERMINT:

A favorite for healing and cleansing spells. Rub the furniture and walls throughout a dwelling to cleanse them of evil.

PERIWINKLE:

This herb is carried to attract money and to dispel the evil eye or evil spirits.

Burn as an incense to help restore lost memories.

Combine with Love incense and burn in your bedroom to increase sexual passions.

PINE:

Sprinkle Pine needles around the floors then sweep to remove evil from your home or business.

Burn as an incense to cleanse your home.

PINE

Sprinkle on your money and in your wallet before going gambling to add money drawing power.

PIPSISSEWA:

Crush and blend with Rose Hips and Violet Flowers. Burn when calling only good spirits for help.

PLAINTAIN:

Hang this herb in a Blue flannel bag inside your car to protect it from envious people who might have evil intent.

PIPSISSEWA

POKE ROOT:

To remove a jinx and protect a business mix Pokeroot with Spearmint and make into a tea. Sprinkle the tea throughout the store. Whatever portion is unused can be kept in a jar to keep away any other jinxing attempts. If you believe that the curse has also been placed on you personally, poor this tea in your bathwater. You will be uncrossed and given a boost of courage to move on.

This combination of herbs can also be burned as an incense to break a hex or curse.

POPPY

POPPY SEEDS:

When seeking to confuse someone, first inscribe their name on a Brown candle. Mix Poppy seeds with Confusion oil and rub onto the candle during the full moon, while saying a prayer to dominate your enemy.

PRIMROSE:

If your child's behavior has gone out of control, put Primrose in his pillowcase and in his bath water, he will then settle down and follow your rules.

PRIMROSE

Q

QUASSIA:

To keep your lover under your power and control, mix Quassia Chips with hair of your mate; and burn to ashes. The ashes are then put in a small jar and mixed with Controlling powder and Cinnamon oil.

Keep Quassia Chips with you at work to have advancement in your career and protection from those envious of your position.

QUEEN OF THE MEADOW:

Excellent for winning at bingo and other types of gambling. Add 4 ounces to gallon of water let it stand for 7 days. Use a pint a day in your bath water.

QUEENS ROOT:

If you are hoping for a marriage proposal from your mate, just prior to seeing him, make a tea from this root and pour it in your bathwater.

Add to Four Thieves Vinegar and use as a floorwash to encourage harmony in the home.

QUINCES:

For protection in any situation, carry these seeds in a Red flannel bag.

QUINA ROJO.

A most famous love herb from Mexico. Boil 1 ounce in 2 quarts of water, add in some Rose Petals. Use 1 cup in your bathwater each day. It is said to make men's heads turn and make their nature run rapid. Only use when sex is desired . Use with extreme caution. Used by prostitutes.

R

RASPBERRY:

This is a personal feminine herb which should only be used by real calm, cool ladies. Add 4 ounces of leaves to 1 gallon of water. Let it sit for 3 days. Use to bring peace and harmony to your marriage. Bathe in it daily, your man will not want to wander.

RATTLE SNAKE ROOT:

Mix with Lovers incense, burn the incense and drink the tea. This is said to attract the right lover and prevent a wrong and unhappy choice.

To stop others from harming you or your children, brew into a tea and mix with bathwater. Also use as a rinse water for your clothing for additional protection.

RHUBARB ROOT:

Cook in with other food and feed to your lover to stop infidelity.

ROCK SALT:

Mix with Dill Seeds and sprinkle around the house to remove jinx.

ROSE HIPS:

Carry in a red bag and love will soon surround you.

RHUBARB

ROSEMARY:

Very good for cleansing baths Add with other herbs such as Ruda, Basil, and Lavendar Make into a tea and use daily for cleansing and protection.

Any time you do a hexing or jinxing spell, wash your hands afterwards with Rosemary tea.

Known to help preserve a youthful look. Mix one pound of Rosemary to 2 gallons of water and leave sit for 3 days (keep it cool) Wash your facewith this mixture morning and night.

Rosemary is powerful in warding off evil. Keep some in your home in a jar or cotton bags. It can also be burnt on charcoal to dispel evil from your home.

To assure faithfulness keep Rosemary near your bed.

Sew into your pillow to ward off nightmares.

Hang over your doors and window sills to keep evil spirits from entering your

ROSEMARY

ROSE PETALS:

Known as a love herb. To keep your relationship strong, place a picture of your lover in a bowl of Rose Petals.

To make your relationship stronger, scatter Rose Petals all over the floor in the bedroom, leave them on the floor during the day and vacuum or sweep them up at night.

Brew a tea with Rose Petals and use in your bath to attract love.

ROSE

Place the picture of the person you wish to attract in a Red flannel bag along with a bunch of Rose Petals. Each time you are going to see the person anoint the bag with Attraction oil.

To remove any hex or jinx, rub your body with Rose Petals after you bathe.

ROWAN WOOD:

One of the oldest protective amulets known is made by tying two Rowan twigs in the shape of a cross using red thread or yarn. Carry with Amber stones in a Red bag anointed with Protection oil.

RUDA:

Ruda added to the bath helps break all types of hexes that have been cast upon you.

Put Ruda in a White flannel bag and hang above the front door to ward off evil spirits.

Make into a tea and sprinkle inside and outside the home for protection to ward off all kinds of illnesses.

RUE:

If you need help functioning mentally after a quarrel with your lover, the scent of Rue will help in clearing your mind.

Rue brewed into a tea and poured in your bathwater is said to be very effective in breaking the influence of any hex or curse that has been cast upon you.

S

RUE

SACRED BARK:

Keep Sacred Bark burning in a bowl on the altar in your ritual room for purification.

Some card readers keep Sacred Bark burning to help them concentrate.

Make an infusion of Sacred Bark. Sprinkle it around your home before going to court, this can help bring a favorable verdict.

Place the following herbs into a White pouch; Buckthorn, Marigold and Sacred Bark, and carry them into court with you for a favorable outcome.

SAFFLOWER:

Used by gay men. Burn on charcoal as an incense. Rub small amounts on the inside of the knees for exciting sexual encounters.

SAGE:

Carry some in a Yellow flannel bag to guard against the dreaded evil eye.

When doing reversible spells mix Sage with Reversible incense.

SALTPETER:

Known also as Vesta powder. Can be fed to men to keep their nature from rising.

If you want to increase the power of any incense mix in some Saltpeter. Use with caution, it is highly flammable.

SAMPSONS SNAKE ROOT:

Carried in a yellow bag and makes one more sexually ready. Can also be used in the bath water.

Rub on the man's private part to help give him an erection.

Make a conjure bag containing a pair of Red lodestones, Heart of a Swallow, some Sampsons Snake Root and carry near your private part.

SAGE

SANDALWOOD:

One of the three holy incenses. Burn on charcoal or use as an oil. Use to help make wishes come true Sandalwood also provides protection and has great healing powers.

Carry some in a Yellow flannel bag to guard against the dreaded evil eye.

SARSAPARILLA:

Drink as a tea or put in your bath water to make you more sexually sensual and excite passions.

Mix with Cinnamon and Sandalwood powder to draw money in a hurry.

Said to be a blood purifier when cooked into your food.

SASSAFRAS:

Should be carried in your purse or wallet near your money, helps you control and make your money go further.

Infused in a tea, Sassafras has a calming effect on the stomach and is said to purify your whole system.

SASSAFRAS

SAW PALMETTO:

To help a man get an erection, mix this herb with Sarsaparilla, Muira Puama and Damiana and make into a strong tea. Helps men get an erection. This is what all the ancient gods used to have sexual encounters.

SCULLCAP:

If your worried that your man is being unfaithful put some Scullcap in a White bag along with 2 White lodestones and sew to your husband's pillow. He'll only have eyes for you.

SCULLCAP

Add to your lover's food to stop infidelity.

SENNA:

When someone doesn't know that you want them. Write their name on parchment paper with doves blood ink, and put Senna leaves, come to me oil in a Yellow flannel bag and carry on your person.

SENNA ROOT:

Make into a tea and let cool. Anoint on mate while sleeping to stop infidelity. May also be added to their food to keep them home.

SHAME WEED:

Dry and pulverize then toss in the path of a debtor to shame them into paying.

SILVERWEED:

Seal in a bottle of whiskey and keep around the house as a potent lucky charm.

SENNA

SLIPPERY ELM:

Use to stop vicious gossip. Burn and the odor will seal the lips of the one who is slandering you. A potent force when used correctly.

SMARTWEED:

Attracts money and clears the mind. Carry in a Green flannel bag along with 4 coins, add Money Drawing powder and anoint weekly with Money Drawing oil.

SNAKEROOT:

Carry this root to have good oluck and be in control of any situation.

SOLOMONS SEAL:

Burn as a special incense for success.

One should always take a bath or carry Solomons Seal for protection.

Brew the roots into a tea and sprinkle around any area that needs protection.

SNAKEROOT

SOUTHERN JOHN THE CONQUEROR ROOT:

To increase sexual passion, add to wash water used for bed sheets and night clothes.

Ground the root into powder and rub the mattress and sprinkle around your bedroom This is said to make a man very horny.

Carry in a Green flannel bag for luck, money and protection.

SPEARMINT:

Mix with Gloria incense and burn to rid your home of demons, ghosts, or evil spirits. Burn at 10 pm for 11 consecutive days.

SPEARMINT

Mix with Balm of Gilead, Barberry, Solomons Seal and Jasmin for cleansing or when someone has done something evil to you.

(continued)

Crush and mix with incense. Burn to attract renters to an empty house or apartment.

SPIKENARD:

To make your love secure. In a flower pot put some Spikenard, some of your own pubic hair and a picture of the one you love. Fill the pot with soil and keep in it your bedroom, water the plant only with Holy Water. Do this once a month to keep your husband or mate from wandering.

Brew into a tea for sprinkling purposes. Wet the picture of a loved one and they will never leave you.

Place the root in a Red chamois bag and wear around you neck to attract good luck.

SPIKENARD

SQUAW VINE:

Pregnant women should bathe in a tea made of this wonderful herb once a week to keep jealousy away from the unborn child.

Squaw Vine and Raspberry Leaves made into a tea help ease labor pains.

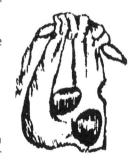

SQUILL ROOT:

To attract new customers brew into a tea and use in a cleaning mixture for washing down a place of business.

(continued)

To draw money. Place some Squill root, one silver dime, one silver quarter and one silver dollar bill in a jar, box or flannel bag. Sprinkle the bag with Money Drawing Powder and anoint with Bayberry oil. While burning Money Drawing Incense and a Green candle say the following money drawing prayer:

"Father and All Saints, I call on you to help me succeed, as I need the money to help me in my life, please I beg of you, help me draw money, bring me silver, bring me dollars hot or cold."

(Anoint the bag, burn the candle and the incense each day until you get the assistance you need.)

STAR ANISE:

Place a bowl of Star Anise on the altar or where you are doing your rituals, to purify and help increase the power. Renew each week.

Carry to bring good luck.

Burn the seeds as an incense to help increase psychic powers.

ST. JOHN'S WORT:

To calm nervousness and anxiety, this herb can be added to boiling water and taken internally. *(Only use under the supervision of a qualified medical professional).*

SULPHUR:

Add to any jinxing or hexing spell. Mix with Asafoetida and War Powder and roll all these ingredients into a black wax ball. Write your enemies name on the wax and throw it into his yard.

This is not an herb, do not use it on anyone's body and NEVER take internally.

SUMBUL ROOT:

A very powerful love herb. Said to attract the opposite sex very quickly. Carry as a charm, burn as an incense or brew into a tea and pour into your bath water.

SWEETPEA:

It is said that if you carry Sweetpea flowers with you wherever you go you will attract friendships and perhaps even love relationships.

T

TANSY

TANSY:

A bit of Tansy placed in your shoes helps to keep the law away. Also bathe in it to keep the law away.

THYME:

Put in a jar and keep in the home for good luck.

Burn as an incense to cleanse magic rooms.

Stuff in pillows to help stop nightmares.

Burn as an incense in the home to attract good health.

THYME

TONKA BEANS:

A favorite Hoodoo charm for good luck. Carry 4 Tonka Beans, a pair of Green lodestones and Gold Magnetic Sand in a Green flannel bag for luck when gambling.

To make wishes come true carry the beans for 18 days *(no more)*. Then on the 18th day they must be left at a church and your wish will come true in 3 days.

(continued)

Carry two Tonka Beans in a Green conjure bag. Moisten them with two or three drops of Money Drawing Oil.

To have less frequent health problems, and to speed up your natural healing process, carry two Tonka Beans in a Green pouch around your neck.

TREFOIL:

Mix with Vervain, Dill Seed and St. Johns Wort to make one of the most powerful defenses or protection charms against any type of witchcraft: Brew into a tea, do not strain. After you take a bath, rinse yourself with this mixture and sprinkle some around your home.

TWITCH GRASS:

To cause trouble and problems for your enemy. On the night of the full moon, use a rusty nail to inscribe the name of your enemy 6 times on the side of a Black candle. Once done, roll the candle in Twitch Grass. Burn this candle in the cemetery, while it is burning chant your desire aloud.

UV

UNICORNROOT:

Carry 2 roots tied together with Yellow string to bring a new love or lover into your life. Anoint the roots daily with Attraction oil.

To keep your lover faithful bind 2 roots together with white thread and hide in your lover's belongings.

UVA URSI:

A tea made of this a said to help you see the future.

Carry Uva Ursi with you to increase your psychic powers.

Burn as an incense to develop psychic powers and to sharpen your perception.

VALERIAN:

VALERIAN

Wrap the Valerian Root and a picture of your mate in tin foil to stop quarreling or fighting. Carry for 3 days and then throw into running water.

To cause an enemy to wreck or have bad luck with his car, simply hide a Valerian Root in the glove compartment.

(continued)

Bring peace to your home by brewing this root as a tea and sprinkling around the premises. Drink the tea to soothe your nerves.

VANILLA:

This comes in a white powder form. A famous love herb. Take a bath with Patchouly soap, then dust your entire body with Vanilla powder.

Mix this into some love incense and burn daily so your mate will always be thinking about you.

VANILLA

VERBENA:

Bathe your children in this herb to help make them learn faster.

Mix with Sandalwood and burn for a jinx removing.

VERBENA (LEMON):

When a marriage is going sour, place a jar of Lemon Verbena behind the wedding pictures with Peaceful Home powder also added to the jar.

Make into a tea a sprinkle all around the house, especially in the bedroom to restore passionate lovemaking.

VERBENA ROOT:

VERBENA

Add a little to a meal and serve. Makes passions quickly rise. A popular aphrodisiac with Voodooists.

VERVAIN:

Carry in a Red pouch to attract love and bring luck to the one who carries it.

Brew into a potent tea and drink some for good luck, success and healing power.

VETIVERT:

Place in cash registers to increase business. Can also be made into a tea and sprinkled in and around the business.

Burn to overcome evil spells.

VERVAIN

VERTIVERT LEAVES:

Overcomes hexes and makes enemies suffer. Use only against those who have hexed you. Burn to overcome the spell of an enemy.

VIOLET:

A love flower. Mix with Lavender for a great love bath.

When someone is ill; bathe them in Violet to help the sickness heal faster.

VIOLET

VIOLET LEAVES:

Pin four Violet leaves in the form of a cross and wear in your shoe. This will give you the power to force others to do your bidding.

VIRGINIA SNAKE ROOT:

Said to be one of the most powerful of all good luck roots. It is very hard to get and very expensive. Once it is in your possession no one can touch it or see it because the luck will vanish.

Carry in a Green flannel bag for good luck in bingo, lottery and any other type of gambling. Anoint weekly with Snake Root oil.

WAHOO BARK:

Used to unhex people. Brew into a tea and anoint the head of a crossed person. Call *"Wahoo"* in a loud voice seven times. For the next seven days the hexed person must add the tea to his bathwater. This will break any hex the person has on them.

WALNUT LEAVES:

Use to hex your enemies. Write your intent on parchment with black ink. Roll the parchment and Walnut Leaves into a black wax ball and throw it into your enemies yard. As the wax melts your enemie's luck will suffer.

WILD CHERRY HERB:

Soak this herb in Peace Water for nine days and then sprinkle all around the home. Guarantees more harmony and love in the household.

WILD YAM HERB:

Soak in plain rainwater for seven days. Wash hands in this water before taking part in healing rituals. Gives the healer more powers.

WILLOW BARK:

Burned during black magic rituals to call for the aid of Satan.

WINTERGREEN:

Bathe your children in Wintergreen to grant them good fortune and luck throughout their lives.

Also to protect your children from evil kids; take a white flannel bag add Wintergreen, 1 Cross of Caravaca, a piece of Camphor, and a picture to St. Michael. Have your child carry this on their person at all times. Anoint weekly with Holy oil.

WITCH GRASS:

Take a bath in Witch Grass, to help you attract a new lover.

Sprinkle this herb on your lover's clothing to keep him/her from wandering.

Grind into a fine powder and use on Voodoo dolls hex somone.

Use in any hexing ritual to enhance power.

WOODRUFF:

This herb is very good for victory in any circumstance. Very good for people who are into sports. Place some in your left shoe before a game, so your team will be victorious.

For any situation in which you need control over another person, simply carry Woodruff with you in a Red flannel bag.

WORMWOOD:

Hang in a White flannel bag on your rear view mirror of your car, to help prevent accidents.

Burn in your home to remove any hexes or curses.

Wormwood is burnt as an incense to call upon the spiritual guides for assistance.

Burn to bring spirits of the dead back and to cast hexes on those you wish to harm.

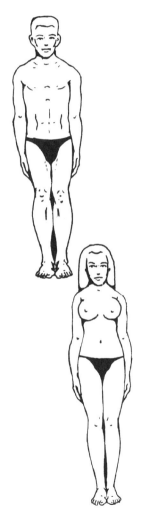

Y

YARROW:

To overcome anxiety in any situation, write your concerns on a piece of parchment paper and put it inside a Yellow flannel bag with some Yarrow. Carry the bag with you to overcome your fears.

YELLOW DUCK ROOT:

Steep into a potent tea and mix with scrub water. Wash the floor to attract business and bring a general change of luck.

YERBA MATE:

To guard against infidelity put 2 tablespoons of Yerbamate into your lover's food once a day.

YERBA MATE

YERBA SANTA:

An ancient recipe said to turn ugly ducklings into beautiful swans. Mix 1 oz. Quince Seed powder and 1 oz. Rose Petals in 2 quarts of water. Boil into a heavy tea. Pour this tea into your bath each day for 7 consecutive days.

YUCCA:

When you do a jinx removing spell use one slice of Yucca root to rub over your entire body. Use a different slice each day for 7 days.

MAGICAL HERBAL RECIPES

ALL PURPOSE 13 HERB BATH

This is the very best of all herbal baths to use!.
It is an ALL PURPOSE bath made up of 13 powerful herbs.

All-purpose mixtures are made of potent combinations of
ingredients and are useful for almost any application
be it love, money, luck, protection, health etc.

INGREDIENTS:

- Earth Smoke
- Eucalyptus
- Fennel Seed
- Flax Seed
- Garlic
- Hibiscus
- Hyssop
- Jasmine
- Irish Moss
- Mace
- Mistletoe
- Orange flower
- Patchuli

Place equal amounts of the ingredients listed above
in a bowl the pour into a stocking as described on
Page 4. Allow the stocking filled with herbs to soak
in your tub of warm water for about 15-20
minutes. Before removing, squeeze the stocking
several times to release the natural essences of the
herbs, then swish it around the tub.

The mixture above can be used (dry) as an incense,
it can be made into a powder to sprinkle around
your home or business or it could be added to wa-
ter and used as floorwash.

SPIRITUAL CLEANSING BATH

This select list of herbs should be mixed in equal parts. Each herb has its own specific influence. Prepared togetherthis bath will cleanse your soul from all negative and disruptive energies and at the same time prepare you to go about your day with the knowledge that you will make the right choices and project positve energy.

INGREDIENTS:

- BASIL
- BAY LEAVES
- HYSSOP
- LETTUCE
- PEPPERMINT
- PARSLEY

- PURSLANE
- ROSE PETALS (WHITE)
- ROSEMARY
- RUE
- SAGE
- VERVAIN

• You can add a few drops of the following oils to this bath to enhance its effects, Lotus Oil, Jasmine Oil and Sandalwood Oil.

• It is also suggested that you burn a White candle while you bathe.

 ## Relieve Stress & Sleep Easy Bath

Soothe your mind, release your tensions. Allow yourself the proper rest so that you can think clearly and function properly for the challenging day ahead. Try to prepare this bath at a quiet time. Put on some peaceful music, take the phone off the hook, and relax.

INGREDIENTS:

- Marjoram
- Chamomile
- Vervain
- Lavender
- Sandalwood
- Peppermint

*(Pregnant women should substitute **Rue** for **Marjoram**)*

 ## Road Opener Bath

This bath should be used by an individual to open up the roads to opportunity and success.

INGREDIENTS:

- Allspice
- Cinnamon
- Clover
- Bay
- Sage
- Kolonia 1800
- Holy Water
- White Candle

1. *Prepare the herbs as described earlier. Store your mixture in a jar (see page 4) for additional baths.*

2. *Add Kolonia 1800 and Holy Water (both available in any Occult Supply shop) to your bathwater.*

3. *Bathe for 15-20 minutes, light the white candle before you climb in the tub.*

4. *Start this bath on Monday and repeat for three consecutive days.*

ENERGY BATH

Get out of the rut that's draining your energy, keeping you from a new relationship or keeping you from advancing your career. Give yourself a boost, jumpstart your progress!

INGREDIENTS:

- LUCKY HAND
- ROSEMARY
- GRAINS OF PARADISE
- FENUGREEK
- GENTIAN
- HIGH JOHN THE CONQUEROR
- MYRTLE
- PEACH

• Anoint a red candle with Passion Oil and burn it while you bathe.

• Store your herbal mixture as described earlier. Repeat this procedure for 7 consecutive days.

 ## TRANQUILITY BATH

This bath brings a person great inner peace and clarity of mind.

- LAVENDER
- SCULLCAP
- VERVAIN
- PEACE WATER
- KOLONIA 1800
- BLUE CANDLE

1. Boil the Lavender, Scullcap and Vervain in 1 quart of water. Allow the mixture to cool and then strain into a large bowl.

2. Add the Peace Water and Kolonia 1800 to the mixture (find these ingredients at an occult supply shop).

3. Pour the mixture into your bathwater, light the blue candle and bathe for 30 minutes. Do this for 3 consecutive nights before going to bed.

MAGICAL HERBAL RECIPES FOR MONEY

MONEY DRAWING BAG

*In a Red pouch, mix equal parts
of each of the following herbs:*

Alfalfa • Mandrake • Jasmine • Golden Seal
Basil • Grains of Paradise • Sesame

*Drop in a Red Clover and tie the bag shut with Green Thread.
Anoint it every day with Money Drawing Oil
and carry it with you to attract money.*

WEALTH DRAWING BAG

In a Green pouch, mix the following ingredients:

1 Orris Root • Nutmeg • Sage • 2 or 3 Cloves
2 Tonka Beans • Alfalfa • Chamomile

*Also add a Jade gemstone and sprinkle
Money Drawing Powder over the blend.
Keep the bag with you at all times.*

BRINGING IN MONEY ON A POWER LEVEL

1. *Cut and hollow out a small hole in the top of a
nutmeg.*

2. *Place mercury into the hole.*

3. *Melt a Green candle over it until it covers e hole
to seal it.*

When you are done, carry it with you.

TO FIND MONEY

Place the following in a Green Mojo Bag:
SMARTWEED • LODESTONE • GOLD MAGNETIC SAND

 ## TO DRAW MONEY

1. *Place a green Lodestone in a red pouch.*
2. *Place a Patchouli herb over it.*
3. *Anoint the bag with Money Drawing Oil.*
4. *Place the bag in a dark place where others will not touch it, for seven days.*
5. *After the seven days, take it out and start to carry it with you. Money will be drawn to you.*

 ## ANOTHER MONEY DRAWING RITUAL

Do this ritual on a Thursday.
In a Green Bag add the following:

FENUGREEK • ORRIS ROOT • CHAMOMILE
SEAL OF PROSPERITY • JADE STONE • MONEY DRAWING POWDER
SOMETHING PERSONAL (HAIR, ETC.)

• *Anoint the bag with Money Drawing Oil.*
• *Burn a Green 7-Day Candle.*
• *Carry the bag with you for 7 days.*

FINANCIAL SUCCESS IN ANY VENTURE

*Use this incense when wishing to obtain success in any venture,
such as business or gambling.*

**FRANKINCENSE • SANDALWOOD • CINNAMON • MYRRH
PATCHOULI LEAVES • ORRIS ROOT POWDER • BENZOIN**

*Mix together these ingredients and burn on charcoal,
until your desire is fulfilled.*

 ## MONEY ATTRACTION BATH

*You can use the following as a bath, or use it as afloorwash or
sprinkling powder in your home or business.
Mix the following ingredients:*

PEPPERMINT • MYRRH • SANDALWOOD • FRANKINCENSE • ROSEMARY

 ## MONEY ATTRACTION INCENSE

Mix the following ingredients and burn on charcoal:

BENZOIN • FRANKINCENSE • SANDALWOOD • SALT PETER • MYRRH

 ## GIVE ME YOUR MONEY ROOT

*Take a Jezebel Root and cover it with wax from a Green candle
and then bury it. This is said to make other spend or give away
their money.*

PRAYER TO THE RUE FOR MONEY

Make an infusion of this herb and sprinkle at your doorway and window frames as you say the following prayer:

"Rue, green and perfumed, wherever you are placed you bring luck. Your secret is as no other and never shall you be in need, there is no other in comparison. You free us from all harm and bring us good fortune. For this reason I await your help, sprinkling your water at my door, for as it is opened, love and money shall enter. Amen."

5 HERBAL BATH

This multi-purpose herbal bath can be used for fast money, bingo luck or to attract love.

ROSEMARY • RUDA • ROSE PETALS • FEVERFEW • ASH LEAVES

Use this herbal combination in your bath water on a daily basis. Use it as a tea to sprinkle around your home or business.

LUCKY DEVIL'S SHOESTRING

This famous Voodoo root is used to draw luck and money. Cut the root into small pieces and place in a jar filled with Four Thieves Vinegar and a block of Camphor. Whenever power is needed, take a piece of the root out and rub it on your body.

MAGICAL HERBAL FORMULAS FOR GAMBLING LUCK

MOJO MONEY BAG

In a green mojo bag carry the following items:

A Small Magnetic Horseshoe
Nutmeg, Alfalfa
Seal of Good Luck, Seal of Fortune
A Parchment Paper folded twice with your name,
a Dollar Sign and a Horseshoe drawn on it.

- *Focus on your intent.*
- *Sprinkle the bag once a week on your astrologically correct day with Success Oil.*
- *Keep this bag with you when you gamble.*

GAMES OF CHANCE

1. *Place a medium to large High John Root in a pot of water and bring to a boil.*

2. *Wash your hands in this water after it cools, before playing lotto, roulette, dice or other games of chance.*

*It helps to wear
Money Drawing Oil, Jasmine Oil,
Sandalwood Oil, Gambler's Oil
or Lodestone Perfume.*

FAMOUS VOODOO SPELL

1. *Drill a hole in a nutmeg.*

2. *Fill the hole with Mercury.*

3. *Seal the hole with the wax of a Green Candle.*

4. *Place the following into either a leather bag or a green mojo bag:*

LUCKY HAND ROOT	GOLD MAGNET SAND
2 GREEN OR NATURAL LODESTONES	HIGH JOHN ROOT
SILVER MAGNET SAND	FIVE FINGER GRASS
ORRIS ROOT	DEVIL'S SHOESTRING ROOT

1. *Place the nutmeg into the bag and sew it shut.*

2. *Sprinkle the bag with Luck Oil at least once a week (on each Thursday and any other time you wish).*

3. *Let no other person touch it.*

4. *Carry this bag at all times when you gamble.*

CARD PLAYERS ONLY

1. *Bring one pint of water with three tablespoons of Chamomile to boiling point, then let simmer on a low flame for about thirty minutes.*

2. *Allow the mixture to cool down, then wash your hands with it just prior to beginning your card game.*

PAPA JIM'S SPECIAL GOOD LUCK INCENSE

Use this incense to have all around good luck in any situation.

ROSE PETALS • ROSEMARY • EUCALYPTUS
COPAL • ANISE STAR

Burn this incense on charcoal.

 ## THE BEST GAMBLING HAND

NUTMEG • MERCURY • GREEN CANDLE • RED BAG • LODESTONE
BLACK CAT BONE • SWALLOW'S HEART • JOHN THE CONQUEROR ROOT
DEVIL SHOESTRING • FIVE FINGER GRASS • JOCKEY CLUB COLOGNE

1. Take a Nutmeg drill a hole in it and pour in pure Mercury.

2. Seal it with wax from a Green candle.

3. Using a Red flannel bag, put a piece of highly
4. Magnetic Lodestone, a Black Cat Bone, Heart of a Swallow, John the Conqueror Root, Devil Shoestring, and some Five Finger Grass.

5. On top of all this place the prepared Nutmeg. When this is done, seal the bag by sewing it all the way around, so that none of the articles fall out.

6. On the outside of the bag sprinkle three drops of Jockey Club Cologne. (Sprinkle once a week)

• Keep this bag on your person at all times.
• Allow no one to touch the bag.

LUCKY BUCKEYE

Carry 4 Buckeyes in a Green flannel bag along with some silver coins. Anoint the bag once a week with Lucky Gamblers oil and carry it with you for good luck and success.

 ## FORTUNE DRAWING

Herbs needed are:
CHAMOMILE • SAGE • MARIGOLD

1. Anoint a one dollar bill, a silver quarter, and a Buckeye first with Bayberry Oil, then Holy Oil and then Money Drawing Oil.

2. Wrap these items in the following manner: Place the silver quarter with the eagle right side up and face down on left side of the dollar (so that it is aligned with the eagle on reverse of the dollar).

3. Sprinkle Power Oil over contents and on the inside seams of the bag.

4. Then place anointed Buckeye on top of the coin and roll the dollar bill from the left to the right so that the All Seeing Eye - Great Seal is showing and fold the ends to make it compact.

5. Tape to ensure it is secure. Place this in a green mojo bag which contains Chamomile, Sage and Marigold herbs along with some additional money.

6. Carry the bag with you.

MAGICAL HERBAL POTIONS FOR LOVE

 ### LOVE CHARM

In a red pouch, carry a little of each herb mixed together.

Couch Grass	2 Tonka Beans	Rose Buds
Vervain	Vanilla Bean	Lavender

Concentrate on what you want as you mix these, then add a little Attraction Powder.

 ### PASSION

Mix the following ingredients as an herbal incense:

1/2 oz. Orris Root powder	1/2 oz. Lavender
1/2 oz. Anise Seed	4 oz. Rose powder
1/4 oz. Saltpeter	1/2 oz. Red Clover

1. Burn self-igniting charcoal until it is burning strongly, then sprinkle the blend over it.

2. Concentrate on your desire.

3. On a piece of white paper using red ink, write the name of the person five times.

4. Then use a match to light it and burn it to ashes in a dish or over the incense.

5. When you have done this, throw it outside to the wind. Do this for seven days. Use two or three drops of Love Oil each morning to achieve the results.

TO GET THE ONE YOU WANT

Take a Mandrake Root and carve the name of the person you wish to attract into the root. As you do this, tell it what you want to be done. Add Red Clover, Rose and a piece of Willow. Wrap all the ingredients in a piece of red satin and place it under your bed.

KEEP YOUR MAN HOME

1. *Place a Rose of Jerico in water and let it open. As soon as it is opened, take it out.*

2. *On a piece of parchment paper write the name of your mate along with your intention.*

3. *Place the Rose of Jerico and the parchment on a picture of you and your mate.*

4. *Pour 1 ounce of Stay at Home Oil and Stay at Home Powder over these items.*

5. *Let the Rose of Jericho dry out, place it in a red satin bag and keep it under your bed.*

BATH TO ATTRACT A NEW LOVER

This bath should make you more appealing to all those you encounter.

SAGE • PEPPERMINT • ANISE STAR • LAVENDAR • ROSE PETALS • SAFFLOWER

•Mix all herbs into 2 quarts of water and boil.
• Strain and place in a jar and use about one half cup per bath.
• Bathe with the mixture for 5 days.

MAKE AN UNWANTED LOVE GO AWAY

Mix some Virginia Snake Root with the person's hair and an article of their clothing. Burn this and that person will leave you alone.

 ## BATH TO ATTRACT A NEW LOVER #2

This bath will make you feel more alive and attractive. The opposite sex will notice!

LAVENDAR • ROSE PETALS • JASMINE • ORANGE FLOWERS RUDA • STAR ANISE • MYRTLE

Mix all the herbs together. Use 1/7 of the mixture in one quart of hot water in the bath, each day, for 7 days straight. After each bath dust your body with Orris Root Powder.

 ## JOHN THE CONQUEROR ROOT LOVE CHARM

If one party is not showing enough affection, perform the following ritual.

1. *Place half a grapefruit in a pan. Add Salt peter, Peppercorns, and Epson Salts.*

2. *Write the desired person's name on parchment, roll it and insert it into the grapefruit.*

3. *Set 9 Pink candles around the pan and light them.*

4. *While the candles are burning, rub a John the Conqueror Root in your hands while circling it around the candles, concentrate on your desire.*

5. *Do this each day for nine consecutive days.*

LOVE PROTECTION HERBAL BATH

This bath is used to protect you and your lover from the eyes of others. It also protects their health and well-being. Mix the following 5 herbs together.

ORRIS ROOT CUT • VIOLET FLOWERS • CLOVES
CHAMOMILE • ROSEMARY

Boil 1 quart and add one seventh of the herb each day to your lover's bath. Do this for 7 consecutive days.

PAPA JIM
LOVE AND ATTRACTION INCENSE

Use this special blend to attract and hold love.

ROSEMARY • LAVENDAR • ROSE PETALS
EUCALYPTUS • SANDALWOOD

BIND YOUR LOVER TO YOU

1. *Take 2 pieces of Rowan Wood. Write your lover's name on one and your name on the other, use Dove's Blood Ink.*

2. *Bind the two pieces together in the shape of a cross with red ribbon.*

3. *Place the cross in a white box and cover it with Guinea Pepper.*

4. *Place the box under your mattress. Your lover will be unable to leave you.*

UNHEXING

MAGICAL HERBAL POTIONS FOR PROTECTION AND JINX REMOVING

 JINX REMOVING

7 HERBAL BATH

*This herbal bath is good for jinx removing,
as an uncrossing bath and as an unhexing bath.*

BASIL • ROSE PETALS • LAVENDER
BAY LEAVES • CHICKWEED • ASH LEAVES • MUGWORT

*This bath is also good for sprinkling. First make into a tea,
then sprinkle. Can also be used as a floorwash.*

 JINX REMOVING

PAPA JIM SPECIAL EVIL AND JINX REMOVING INCENSE

*Use this incense when you feel you have been jinxed.
Burn it on charcoal.*

EUCALYPTUS • ROSEMARY • CASCARA SAGRADA • RED SANDALWOOD

Burn everyday for faster results.

 STOP EVIL

THE THREE HOLY INCENSE

FRANKINCENSE • MYRRH • SANDALWOOD

*Combine these three herbs in powder form and burn as an
incense to remove any type of jinx or evil intent.*

SAHUMERIO COMPUESTO

This is a special mixture of herbs used to remove and cleanse your home of evil, jinx, or curses. Use as an incense on charcoal.

GARLIC SKINS • ROSEMARY • SANDALWOOD
EUCALYPTUS • CINNAMON • ANISE STAR

SEVEN HOLY SPIRIT HYSSOP BATH

This product is sold in most occult supply shops. It is a cleansing bath to remove jinx, hexes or curses. Pour one ounce into the bath water and say the following:

"Purge me with the holy hyssop, and I shall be cleansed, wash me with the hyssop, and I shall be whiter than snow."

This bath is more effective when taken 7 days in succession, or every other day for 14 days. While taking this bath keep a Holy Spirit Candle burning.

PROTECTION BAG

Combine the following herbs in a Purple bag:

ACACIA • HIGH JOHN THE CONQUEROR ROOT • CINNAMON

Anoint each day with Protection Oil and carry with you at all times.

COMMONLY USED HERBS
ENGLISH - SPANISH

Adder's Tongue - *Lengua de Vibora*
Almond - *Almendra*
Angelica - *Arcangel*
Anise - *Anis*
Ash Tree - *Fresno*
Aster - *Amelo*
Balm - *Abejera*
Barberry - *Acetin*
Barley - *Cebada*
Basil - *Albahaca*
Bearberry - *Gayuba*
Bethel Nut - *Areca*
Betony - *Betónica*
Birch - *Abedul*
Bittersweet - *Dulcamara*
Blackberry - *Zarzamora*
Blood Root - *Sangrinaria*
Blueberry - *Arándano*
Borage - *Borraja*
Buckthorn - *Aladierna*
Buckwheat - *Yerba Acre*
Bugle - *Pinillo Rastrero*
Burdock - *Bardana*
Cabbage - *Col*
Cactus Family - *Nolales*
Calamus - *Acoro*
Camphor - *Alcanfor*
Caraway - *Alcaravea*
Cashew - *Acaju*
Catnip - *Gatera*
Celandine - *Celidonia*
Centaury - *Abre-puno*
Chamomile - *Manzanilla*
Cherry - *Cerezas*
Chick Peas - *Garbanzos*
Chickweed - *Alsine*
Chicory - *Achicoria*
Cinnamon - *Canela*
Clove - *Clavo*
Coltsfoot - *Una de Caballo*
Comfrey - *Pulmonaria*
Coriander - *Cilantro*
Cornflower - *Aciano*

Cotton - *Algodonero*
Cumin - *Comino*
Cypress - *Ciprés*
Damiana - *Venado*
Dandelion - *Amargon*
Dill - *Aneto*
Dogwood - *Palo Emborrachador*
Dragon Blood - *Palo de Pollo / Sangre de Dragon*
Ebony - *Abenuz*
Elder - *Sauco*
Elecampane - *Altabaca*
Eucalyptus - *Eucalipto*
Eyebright - *Eufrasia*
Fennel - *Hinojo*
Fenugreek - *Alholva / Fenogreco*
Feverfew - *Arugas / Marticaria*
Fig - *Higos*
Fir - *Abeto*
Flax Seed - *Lino*
Fumitory - *Fumaria*
Galangal - *Galanga*
Garlic - *Ajo*
Gentian - *Genciana*
Ginger - *Gengibre*
Goldenrod - *Vara de Oro*
Hellebore - *Eleboro Fetido*
Heliotrope - *Alacrancillo*
Henbane - *Beleño Negro*
Henna - *Alcana*
Holly - *Acebo*
Hops - *Lupulo*
Horehound - *Marrubio*
Horsetail - *Cola de Caballo*
Hyacinth - *Jacinto*
Hyssop - *Hisopo*
Iceland Moss - *Liquen Islandico*
Jasmine - *Jasin / Jazin*
Job's Tears - *Acacoyol*
Knotgrass - *Altamandria*
Lavendar - *Alhucema*
Lemon - *Limon*
Lemon Grass - *Limoncillo*

Lettuce - *Lechuga*
Lilac - *Lilas*
Lily - *Azucena*
Lime Wood - *Palo de Cidra*
Linseed - *Lino*
Maidenhair - *Culantrillo*
Male Fern - *Helecho Macho*
Maple - *Arce*
Marigold - *Caléndula*
Marjoram - *Mejorana*
Mistletoe - *Muerdago*
Monkshood - *Acónito*
Mugwort - *Altamisa*
Mulberry - *Moral*
Mullein - *Gordolobo*
Mustard Seed - *Mostaza*
Myrrh - *Mirra*
Myrtle - *Arrayan*
Narcissus - *Narcisco*
Nettle - *Achume / Ortiga*
Nutmeg - *Nuez Moscada*
Oak - *Encina*
Oat - *Avena*
Onion - *Cebolla*
Orange - *Naranjo*
Orange Flower - *Azahar*
Pansy - *Pensamiento*
Parsley - *Apio/ Perejil*
Parsnip - *Bastardilla*
Peach - *Alberchigo*
Penny Royal - *Poleo*
Peony - *Peonia*
Peppermint - *Menta*
Pine - *Pino*
Pine Needles - *Alhumajo*
Plaintain - *Llanten*
Primrose - *Oreja de Oso*
Poplar - *Alamo*

Poppy - *Ababol*
Purslane - *Verdolaga*
Quassia - *Quacia Amarga*
Queen of the Meadow - *Ulmaria*
Quince - *Membrilos*
Rhubarb - *Ruibarbo*
Rose - *Rosla*
Rosemary - *Romero*
Rue - *Ruda*
Salflower - *Cartamo*
Sage - *Salvia*
Sarsaparilla - *Zarzaparrilla*
Sassafras - *Sasafras*
Senna - *Sen*
Squill - *Albarranilla*
Sulphur - *Alcribite*
Star Anise - *Badiana*
Vervain - *Verbena*
Scullcap - *Escrofularia Laterales*
Snake Root - *Escoba de la Vibora*
Snakeweed - *Bistorta*
Sorrel - *Romaza Vejigosa*
St. John's Wort - *Hipericón*
Sunflower - *Girasol*
Sweet Flag - *Calamo*
Sweet Pea - *Alverjilla*
Thyme - *Serpol / Tomillo*
Tumerio - *Curcuma*
Turnip - *Nabo*
Valerian - *Valeriana*
Violet - *Anoda*
Walnut - *Nogal*
Willow - *Jara*
Wormwood - *Ajenjo*
Wolfbane - *Aconito / Raiz del Diablo*
Wood Sorrel - *Acetosilla*
Yarrow - *Altarreina*

COMMONLY USED HERBS
SPANISH - ENGLISH

Ababol - Poppy
Abedul - Birch
Abejera - Balm
Abenuz - Ebony
Abeto - Fir
Abre-puno - Centaury
Acacoyol - Job's Tears
Acaju - Cashew
Acebo - Holly
Acetin - Barberry
Acetosilla - Wood Sorrel
Achicoria - Chicory
Achume / Ortiga - Nettle
Aciano - Cornflower
Acónito - Monkshood
Acoro - Calamus
Ajenjo - Wormwood
Ajo - Garlic
Aladierna - Buckthorn
Alamo - Poplar
Albahaca - Basil
Albarranilla - Squill
Alberchigo - Peach
Alcana - Henna
Alcanfor - Camphor
Alcaravea - Caraway
Alacrancillo - Heliotrope
Alcribite - Sulphur
Algodonero - Cotton
Alholva / Fenogreco - Fenugreek
Alhucema - Lavender
Alhumajo - Pine Needles
Almendra - Almond
Alsine - Chickweed
Alverjilla - Sweet Pea
Altabaca - Elecampane
Altamandria - Knotgrass
Altamisa - Mugwort
Altarreina - Yarrow
Amargon - Dandelion
Amelo - Aster
Aneto - Dill
Anis - Anise

Anoda - Violet
Apio/ Perejil - Parsley
Arándano - Blueberry
Arcangel - Angelica
Arce - Maple
Areca - Bethel Nut
Arrayan - Myrtle
Arugas / Marticaria - Feverfew
Avena - Oat
Azahar - Orange Flower
Azucena - Lily
Badiana - Star Anise
Bardana - Burdock
Bastardilla - Parsnip
Betónica - Betony
Bistorta - Snakeweed
Borraja - Borage
Calamo - Sweet Flag
Caléndula - Marigold
Canela - Cinnamon
Cartamo - Salflower
Cebada - Barley
Cebolla - Onion
Celidonia - Celandine
Cerezas - Cherry
Cilantro - Coriander
Ciprés - Cypress
Clavo - Clove
Col - Cabbage
Cola de Caballo - Horsetail
Comino - Cumin
Culantrillo - Maidenhair
Curcuma - Tumerio
Dulcamara - Bittersweet
Eleboro Fetido - Hellebore
Encina - Oak
Escoba de la Vibora - Snake Root
Escrofularia Laterales - Scullcap
Eucalipto - Eucalyptus
Eufrasia - Eyebright
Fresno - Ash Tree
Fumaria - Fumitory
Galanga - Galangal

Garbanzos - Chick Peas
Gatera - Catnip
Gayuba - Bearberry
Genciana - Gentian
Gengibre - Ginger
Girasol - Sunflower
Gordolobo - Mullein
Higos - Fig
Hinojo - Fennel
Hipericón - St. John's Wort
Hisopo - Hyssop
Jacinto - Hyacinth
Jara - Willow
Jasin / Jazin - Jasmine
Lechuga - Lettuce
Lengua de Vibora - Adder's Tongue
Lilas - Lilac
Limon - Lemon
Limoncillo - Lemon Grass
Lino - Flax Seed
Lino - Linseed
Liquen Islandico - Iceland Moss
Llanten - Plaintain
Lupulo - Hops
Manzanilla - Chamomile
Marrubio - Horehound
Mejorana - Marjoram
Membrilos - Quince
Menta - Peppermint
Mirra - Myrrh
Moral - Mulberry
Mostaza - Mustard Seed
Muerdago - Mistletoe
Nabo - Turnip
Naranjo - Orange
Narcisco - Narcissus
Nogal - Walnut

Nolales - Cactus Family
Nuez Moscada - Nutmeg
Oreja de Oso - Primrose
Palo de Cidra - Lime Wood
Palo de Pollo /
Sangre de Dragon - Dragon Blood
Palo Emborrachador - Dogwood
Pensamiento - Pansy
Peonia - Peony
Pinillo Rastrero - Bugle
Pino - Pine
Poleo - Penny Royal
Pulmonaria - Comfrey
Quacia Amarga - Quassia
Raiz del Diablo - Wolfbane
Romaza Vejigosa - Sorrel
Romero - Rosemary
Rosla - Rose
Ruda - Rue
Ruibarbo - Rhubarb
Salvia - Sage
Sangrinaria - Blood Root
Sasafras - Sassafras
Sauco - Elder
Sen - Senna
Serpol / Tomillo - Thyme
Ulmaria - Queen of the Meadow
Una de Caballo - Coltsfoot
Valeriana - Valerian
Vara de Oro - Goldenrod
Venado - Damiana
Verbena - Vervain
Verdolaga - Purslane
Yerba Acre - Buckwheat
Zarzamora - Blackberry
Zarzaparrilla - Sarsaparilla

Item #222
$11.95

THE PSALM WORKBOOK

by Robert Laremy

Work with the Psalms to
Empower, Enrich and Enhance Your Life!

This LARGE PRINT King James version of the Book of Psalms contains nearly 400 simple rituals and procedures that can be used to help you accomplish anything you desire. Use the situational index provided to decide which psalm to pray for your specific need.

Peace, Protection, Health,
Success, Money, Love,
Faith, Inspiration, Spiritual Strength
And much more!

Approach your worship with a clean heart and a child-like faith in God's infinite wisdom and you will derive tremendous results from the powers of the psalms.

MAGICAL RITUALS FOR
PROTECTION
By
DONNA ROSE

Item# 421
$7.95

MAGICAL RITUALS FOR
PROTECTION
by Donna Rose

Oils, Incense & Powders for Protection
Magical Herbs for Protection
Magical Gemstones for Protection
Psalms for Protection
Prayers for Protection

Magical Spells for Protection

Cleansing Ritual
Purification Spell to Cleanse Yourself
Repelling Negativity
To Annul an Evil Spell
Defeat an Enemy's Evil
Binding Someone Annoying Spell
Reversing Spell to Send Back a Curse or Hex
Dragons Blood Reed Spell To Lift Hexes and Jinxes
Overcome an Enemy
Cast Off The Influence Of The Evil Eye
Spell Against Hoodoos Haunts and Evil Works
Spell to Make Someone Move Away